Historical Association Studies

Franklin D. Roosevelt

D0800554

Historical Association Studies

General Editors: Muriel Chamberlain and James Shields

China in the Twentieth Century
Paul Bailey

The Ancien Régime
Peter Campbell

Decolonization
The Fall of the European Empires
M. E. Chamberlain

Gandhi
Antony Copley

The Counter-Reformation
N. S. Davidson

British Radicalism and the French Revolution 1789–1815
H. T. Dickinson

From Luddism to the First Reform Bill
Reform in England 1810–1832
J. R. Dinwiddy

Radicalism in the English Revolution 1640–1660
F. D. Dow

Revolution and Counter-Revolution in France 1815–1852
William Fortescue

The New Monarchy
England, 1471–1534
Anthony Goodman

The French Reformation
Mark Greengrass

Politics in the Reign of Charles II
K. H. D. Haley

Occupied France
Collaboration and Resistance 1940–1944
H. R. Kedward

Appeasement
Keith Robbins

Franklin D. Roosevelt
Michael Simpson

Britain's Decline
Problems and Perspectives
Alan Sked

The Cold War
Joseph Smith

Bismarck
Bruce Waller

The Russian Revolution 1917–1921
Beryl Williams

The Historical Association, 59a Kennington Park Road, London SE11 4JH

Franklin D. Roosevelt

MICHAEL SIMPSON

Basil Blackwell

Copyright © Michael Simpson 1989

First published 1989

Basil Blackwell Ltd
108 Cowley Road, Oxford, OX4 1JF, UK

Basil Blackwell Inc.
3 Cambridge Center
Cambridge, MA 02142, USA

British Library Cataloguing in Publication Data
A CIP catalogue record for this book is available from the British Library.

Library of Congress Cataloging in Publication Data
Simpson, Michael.
    Franklin D. Roosevelt / Michael Simpson.
        p.   cm.—(Historical Association studies)
    Bibliography: p.
    Includes Index
    ISBN 0–631–15284–9
    1.   Roosevelt, Franklin D. (Franklin Delano). 1882–1945.
2.   Presidents—United States—Biography.   3.   New Deal, 1933–
1939. 4.   United States—Politics and government—1933–1945.
I.   Title.   II.   Series.
E807.S5   1989
973.917 0924—JC19

Typeset in 10 on 11½pt Erhardt by Footnote Graphics, Warminster, Wilts
Printed in Great Britain by Whitstable Litho Ltd., Whitstable, Kent

Contents

Acknowledgements   vi

1 A Preface to Power (1882–1928)   1

2 The Road to the White House (1928–1933)   15

3 The New Deal (1933–1945)   23

4 Roosevelt and World Affairs (1933–1945)   50

Conclusion   78

References   81

Notes on Further Reading   84

Index   88

Acknowledgements

Particular thanks are due to the British Academy, Franklin and Eleanor Roosevelt Institute and the University College of Swansea for research funding. I am very grateful for the unfailing assistance, cheerfulness and friendship of Dr William Emerson and the staff of the Franklin D. Roosevelt Library, Hyde Park, New York. Dr Emerson, Professors W. F. Kimball and E. A. Rosen, Dr A. J. Badger and Mr G. C. Ward have commented critically, and to my immense benefit, on the manuscript. My New Deal students at Swansea since 1971 have taught me far more than they can imagine. My family has 'lived with' FDR for many years; I am grateful to them for bearing with my preoccupation.

Michael Simpson

1 A Preface to Power (1882–1928)

Heritage and Environment, 1882–1910

Springwood, the Roosevelt home at Hyde Park on the left bank of the Hudson, eighty-five miles north of New York City, is a modest country house set in woodland. In this haven of peace and security, Franklin Delano Roosevelt was born on 30 January 1882. FDR's father, James (1828–1900), of Dutch ancestry, had acquired Springwood in 1867. A patrician rentier, capitalist, grand tourist, cultivated squire, and a mild and patient man, he was a widower when he married the beautiful, strong-willed Sara Delano (1854–1941) in 1880. She too came from a prosperous Hudson Valley family.

This stable, comfortable and verdant background profoundly influenced FDR's career. 'Hyde Park provided FDR with a set of values that were not necessarily in the mainstream of American life' (Morgan, 1985, p. 36), and his gentlemanly upbringing contrasted starkly with the privations of most of his contemporaries. 'A child of the country', he considered cities 'a perhaps necessary nuisance' (Tugwell, 1969, p. 24). He never really understood businessmen ('He never met a payroll,' they complained during the New Deal) or labour unionists (Perkins, 1947). A 'gentleman farmer' (there was no dirt under his fingernails), he retained a Jeffersonian belief in the farmer as America's backbone and gave agricultural recovery priority in the New Deal (Romasco, 1983). Taught to respect and assist nature, he planted 300,000 trees at Springwood, and as President viewed the nation as an enlarged estate to be conserved. Hyde Park was an oasis of tranquillity in a turbulent society, and, not being a member of a major socio-economic group, FDR was able to avoid total commitment to any single interest and to consider problems with relative detachment.

1

Roosevelt was brought up to be polite, dutiful, reticent and self-reliant. Family circumstances added other traits which featured prominently in his political behaviour. From 1890, his father was a semi-invalid, and FDR and his mother entered into 'a loving conspiracy' not to agitate him (Ward, 1985, pp. 144–5). Franklin learned stoicism in the face of injury or disappointment, telling his parents what they wanted to hear and hiding his true feelings. In escaping from his formidable mother's control, he became devious. Possessing a placid nature and lacking in introspection, he had a 'religious certitude', which, Ward notes (p. 157), enabled him to make hard decisions without worrying about them. Thanks to his 'robust spiritual health' (Tugwell, 1969, p. 31), Roosevelt slept well while the world tossed to and fro.

Young Roosevelt travelled extensively in Europe and was interested in natural history and philately but 'sailing was his passion' (Freidel, 1952, p. 28) and he quickly became a proficient yachtsman and navigator. 'The sea held a rare fascination for him' (Freidel, 1952, p. 28), and he collected naval art and literature, but his father refused to let him join the Navy, insisting that he should succeed to the family estate and investments. It is difficult to see FDR submitting to the genteel poverty, slow promotion, boring routine and lengthy absence on forgotten stations which were the lot of the contemporary naval officer. Nevertheless, he formed a lifelong attachment to the Navy, which he came to treat as a personal fief.

Tutored by governesses and short of playmates, FDR went to school only at fourteen, his over-protective parents sending him in 1896 to Groton in Massachusetts. Roosevelt was unprepared for this stern and competitive boarding school, but with his characteristic eagerness to please and stubborn persistence he adjusted well enough to become a reasonable scholar and moderately acceptable to his schoolfellows. Groton was followed in 1900 by Harvard, a much freer environment. FDR did not extend himself academically and achieved the expected middling grades. His one major attainment was an undistinguished editorship of the student newspaper, *The Crimson*, and he graduated from Harvard in 1904 with little more than strong social and sentimental associations. FDR was, in fact, largely self-educated through his hobbies, environmental observations, eclectic reading and, above all, conversation with all manner of folk.

Qualifying (without distinction) for the New York Bar at Columbia, he joined a conservative Wall Street practice in 1907. While he served his clerkship in desultory fashion, his life centred round the city's social whirl and sailing. He seemed destined to become a carbon copy of his father – a leisured country gentleman. However, spirited and determined, he secretly courted his distant cousin Eleanor (1884–1962) from 1903. Aged nineteen, she was the niece of Theodore Roosevelt (1858–1919; President, 1901–1909) and had experienced a harsh childhood. The tall, lithe and attractive Franklin offered this gangling, shy girl security and overdue happiness. The bargain was not, however, one-sided. Like most Americans, Franklin was swept up in the excitement of TR's brilliant career and may have entertained vague notions of emulating his older cousin. As Ward (1985, p. 315) observes, Eleanor's 'closeness to the man he admired most on earth must have been an important part of her dowry.' The marriage, which took place in 1905, demonstrated FDR's skills in deception and manipulation in the face of his mother's obstruction. 'All the rest of her days she fought a veiled but intense battle to retain possession of Franklin' (Morgan, 1985, p. 21) – to Eleanor's chagrin. Spared the necessity of working to support his family, FDR seemed unconcerned about his future. His mother preferred him to remain at Hyde Park in semi-indolence, and though he is said to have told his fellow law clerks in 1907 that he intended to follow TR's path to the White House, he took few steps to do so.

Baptism in Politics, 1910–1913

FDR entered politics in 1910 on the initiative of Hudson Valley Democratic leaders who were looking for a self-financing candidate for the district's normally Republican State Senate seat. FDR accepted eagerly, probably because an election offered infinitely more excitement than the law. He had few cards to play. His philosophy, in so far as he had one, was his father's Grover Cleveland Democracy – honesty and economy in government – and he was unversed in current issues. He had little standing in the community and no acquaintance with political rough-and-tumble. Even his purse was more limited than his promoters had anticipated. In his favour were a national swing to the Democrats and local dissatisfaction with the incumbent Republican and his conservative party. FDR also had the enthusiasm, vigour and confidence of youth, a handsome profile and a capacity to learn the political

3

ropes with remarkable speed. In a flamboyant campaign, long on energy, short on policies, his inherent opposition to bossism coincided with the current public mood, and he had the sense to concentrate on Republican and uncommitted voters. His first campaign set the pattern for his career. Trading unashamedly on his connection with TR (a Republican), on whom he consciously modelled himself, for the first time he had to appeal to and associate with a broad cross-section of his fellow citizens, and he came home, ahead of his party, in a 'Democratic avalanche' (Freidel, 1952, p. 94).

Roosevelt, still only half committed to politics, displayed little flair for the legislative side, though he was a diligent if unremarkable apprentice State Senator. He ingratiated himself with his constituents and adopted a moderately positive progressivism, the reformist liberalism of the day associated with TR and the rising Democratic star, Governor Woodrow Wilson of New Jersey. Never running far ahead of public opinion, he committed himself to female suffrage and other electoral reforms, the improvement of working conditions, aid to farmers and the conservation of natural resources. Though he chaired the State Senate's Forest, Fish and Game Committee, he never etched his name on significant legislation and might have faded back into gentlemanly idleness after one or two undistinguished terms. A fortuitous issue in 1911 gave him a slightly undeserved prominence on which he capitalized. The Democratic state bosses, working through the Tammany Hall organization in New York City, nominated one of their associates, William 'Blue-Eyed Billy' Sheehan, for the US Senate. Before 1914, US Senators were selected by state legislatures, and the Tammany 'sachems', having solid majorities in both houses of the New York Assembly, anticipated Sheehan's endorsement. Upstate Democrats, traditionally hostile to Tammany and fired by the Progressive crusade for clean government, objected to boss dictation. Roosevelt was drawn naturally and politically to the insurgency and, since his ample Albany home offered a convenient headquarters, he became its spokesman. The rebellion failed after several months, Tammany forcing a marginally more acceptable candidate on the rebels and exacting its revenge when they came up for re-election in 1912. The swansong of many fellow insurgents, the Sheehan fight was the making of FDR's career. He was the one beneficiary of the fight. Reasonably safe from Tammany vengeance, he had emerged as a nationally known upstate Democratic leader of the 'good

4

'government' forces; the fight gave him 'an accelerated course in politics' (Rollins, 1962, p. 32) and revealed his talent for amicable press relations. Moreover, he had visited Wilson in 1911 and come away an early supporter of the Governor's Presidential bid in 1912. Since Tammany could block his ambitions in New York, he had to open up an avenue to national politics. The irony of the Sheehan fight, Morgan (1985) suggests, was that Tammany was undergoing a house-cleaning and often supported Progressive causes. FDR appeared more conservative than the organization and, inadvertently, anti-Catholic, a damaging label in New York.

FDR campaigned strenuously for Wilson in New York in 1912, though with negligible effect. When his own re-election campaign came round, he was down with a fever and called upon a middle-aged, marginally successful political reporter from Albany, Louis Howe, to conduct it. Howe, an untidy, chain-smoking, asthmatic little man was 'a skilled, reliable political amanuensis' (Rollins, 1962, p. 62) and had met Roosevelt during the insurgency. An experienced, scheming, cynical, waspish, witty gnome-like figure, Howe spent heavily on publicity, proclaiming Roosevelt as the friend of farmers and labour and the champion of clean government. Aided by a Republican split and his assiduous cultivation of his constituency, FDR once again ran ahead of his party, increasing his majority. Howe's triumph made him indispensable. 'After 1912 it would be impossible to think of either Roosevelt or Howe without each other' (Rollins, 1962, p. 61). Howe played up to FDR's growing conviction that he was a future President, and he became FDR's manager with the White House as his ultimate goal. Uncouth, jealous, an intriguer and at times over-elaborate, Howe sought only the reflected glory of his hero, to whom he was devoted. It was a well-nigh perfect political partnership, saving Roosevelt from many blunders, for Howe was 'the "no" man from whom the boss could never quite escape' (Rollins, 1962, p. 453).

In his brief second term, Roosevelt headed the Agriculture Committee but left for Washington before he could frame significant legislation. His two years' political apprenticeship were more important for himself than for the state. 'No one who saw him in those years,' recalled Frances Perkins (1947, p. 13), then a lobbyist for social reform at Albany and later Roosevelt's Secretary of Labor, 'would have been likely to think of him as a potential President of the USA.' Her unflattering impression of him as 'tall and slender, very active and alert ... not particularly charming (that came later), artificially serious of face, rarely smiling ... an appearance of looking down his nose at most people' (p. 14) was widely shared. The young Roosevelt had an air of 'patrician superiority and youthful disdain' (Tugwell, 1969, p. 75). He was adroit, energetic, bland and unoriginal, his political testament (a speech at Troy, NY, in March 1912) being an unremarkable homily on the virtues of clean government, the greatest happiness of the greatest number, business–government co-operation and a vague call for national planning. However, he was a winner, he had the nation's best-known surname, a distinctive campaigning style, boundless energy, his cousin's toothy smile, and the invaluable Louis Howe. He had learned quickly, made few mistakes, capitalized on opportunities and emulated TR's first steps to the White House.

Introduction to Government, 1913–1920

Roosevelt's prominence in New York and his early support for Wilson earned him a junior post in the administration. He sought the Assistant Secretaryship of the Navy because TR had held it (1897–8) and because it offered vicarious naval service. Proxies probably made soundings on his behalf (Morgan, 1985; Schlesinger, 1956), and the new Secretary of the Navy, the North Carolinian Josephus Daniels, recalled from the 1912 convention the 'singularly attractive and honorably courageous young Democratic leader' from New York who was familiar with nautical matters (Daniels, 1963, p. 4). In March 1913, a well rehearsed Roosevelt accepted Daniels's offer with hearty alacrity, the press noting the parallel with TR.

Roosevelt's subsequent behaviour reflected his immaturity. 'Like a romantic boy in his love for the Navy', he had 'a callow preoccupation with his own importance' (Rollins, 1962, pp. 88, 121), exulting in the pomp of office – salutes, reviews, exercises and inspections. A disciple of Admiral Mahan and TR, he was, to the delight of most admirals, a 'Big Navy' man and their willing spokesman. 'Let us learn to trust to the judgment of the real experts, the naval officers,' he told a 1915 audience during the 'Preparedness' campaign organized by East Coast leaders, of which he was an early adherent (*Army and Navy Journal*, 22 May 1915). Fearing a German invasion of the western hemisphere, the Preparedness movement demanded naval expansion (some called for 'a

Navy second to none'), a million-man reserve army and universal military service. 'The country needs the truth about the Army and Navy instead of a lot of soft mush about everlasting peace which so many statesmen are handing out to a gullible public,' FDR wrote, implicitly condemning Wilson, Secretary of State Bryan and Daniels (Letters, II, 1948, p. 256). Though the spectres raised by the Preparedness advocates were absurd, Wilson adopted Preparedness in 1916 for electoral and diplomatic reasons, and Daniels persuaded Congress to vote a vast naval expansion. FDR encouraged fellow yachtsmen to prepare themselves and their boats for coastal patrols, sponsored a volunteer training cruise and established an effective Naval Reserve. Instrumental in founding a Council of National Defense (August 1916) to co-ordinate defence production and mobilization, he failed to secure a State–Army–Navy policy committee; military commanders remained ignorant of government policies until required suddenly to implement them.

In crises with Japan and Mexico in 1913, he manifested an ill-considered belligerence. Eager to emulate TR's Spanish–American War exploits (1898), he noted in July 1913 that Mexico 'is the only place just now where there is real action' (Letters, II, 1948, p. 207), at one flashpoint barking, 'It's war – and we're ready!' (Freidel, 1952, p. 231); Wilson's acceptance of mediation disappointed him. Sharing TR's patronizing moralism towards endemic Caribbean political instability, he enthused about the Navy's protectorates established under Theodore's corollary to the Monroe Doctrine (to ensure 'orderly progress' and the fulfilment of international obligations). Following the outbreak of the First World War in 1914, FDR identified with the Allies, despite Wilson's neutrality. Exclaiming early in 1915, 'I just *know* I shall do some awful unneutral thing before I get through!' (Letters, II, 1948, p. 267), he was 'without doubt the least neutral official in all Washington' (Tugwell, 1969, p. 99). He excoriated the administration's timid diplomacy and strategic blindness, assisting Republicans to attack his own side.

Amazingly, Daniels retained the bumptious, disloyal, disruptive Roosevelt, so different in background, temperament, age and interests from himself. However, they were complementary and 'made a good team' (Eleanor Roosevelt, 1949, p. 22). Daniels, a country editor, teetotaller, Methodist and old political hand, dressed quaintly, hastened slowly and gripped firmly the reins of power. A quasi-pacifist, he was appointed because the like-minded Wilson valued his political counsel. Daniels sought to modernize, civilize and democratize naval life, arousing the contempt of most officers. Never entirely comfortable in his berth, he was an exasperating procrastinator and devoid of strategic insight. 'J.D. is too damned slow for words,' Roosevelt complained, and when Europe went to war in 1914, he observed: 'Mr. Daniels totally fails to grasp the situation' and 'he is bewildered by it all, very sweet but very sad!' (Letters, II, 1948, pp. 233, 243, 339). Nevertheless, Daniels gave the Navy an honest, reforming administration and displayed considerable political finesse. Well aware of FDR's infidelity and mimicry of his country ways, Daniels exhibited an astonishing avuncular patience and a genuine liking for the young aristocrat. FDR made up for Daniels's nautical deficiencies, giving the Democratic administration a measure of credibility in the eyes of the conservative officer corps. When Roosevelt matured fully in the 1920s, 'What he spoke slightingly of at first, he came to admire inordinately' (Eleanor, Letters, II, 1948, p. xviii) and acknowledged his debt to Daniels's astute political tutelage and indulgence. 'Josephus Daniels and Louis McHenry Howe should jointly be credited with developing in FDR a maturity and an outlook which might easily not have existed without their influence' (Elliott Roosevelt, Letters, II, 1948, p. xiv).

Howe was Roosevelt's troubleshooter and political handyman. Persuaded by Howe to cultivate the navy yard unions, Roosevelt courted them so successfuly that scarcely any dispute got out of hand, and he earned a sheaf of encomiums from labour leaders. Much of Roosevelt's time was taken up with the equally delicate handling of favour-seeking Congressmen, but, significantly, Howe was absent when in 1914, on bad advice from anti-Tammany leaders, Franklin impulsively fought a Tammanyite in the primary election to select the Democratic candidate for the US Senate. Despite a characteristically vigorous campaign, he was trounced and thereafter co-existed with Tammany in an uneasy truce.

Roosevelt was a capable if not outstanding administrator who got his 'fingers into about everything', although Daniels allowed him little scope to make policy. He found his work 'absorbing' and 'seemed to live at the office'. Acknowledging that he would 'have to work like a new turbine to master this job', within a week he was '*beginning* to catch on' (Letters, II, 1948, pp. 199, 200, 228). He really came into his own when America went to war in April 1917. FDR 'demonstrated an ability to get things done when the nation placed an almost hysterical premium upon that trait' (Freidel, 1952, p. 318) and he and Howe cut red tape, commandeered supplies and expedited production. Under Roosevelt's supervision, a training camp in New York for 7,000 men took six and a half weeks from the site inspection to occupation. FDR had grasped the likely magnitude and duration of 'the most terrible drama in history' (Letters, II, 1948, p. 237) and the probability of American intervention as early as 1914. Now, recognizing the imperatives of total war, he was 'inexpressibly busy' combating the 'old lady officers and lack of decision in the Department' (Letters, II, 1948, pp. 352, 362). He may well have saved Daniels by sponsoring an independent report on the Department which was sent to Wilson, who persuaded Daniels to move faster and promote younger officers to key posts. Like Winston Churchill at the Admiralty, FDR pressed pet schemes of doubtful utility, such as the construction of several hundred undersized submarine chasers. Nevertheless, he saw that the defeat of the German submarine campaign to starve Britain into surrender by the autumn of 1917 was a major key to victory, and urged the dispatch of all available anti-submarine craft. He adopted a plan for a North Sea mine and net barrage to prevent the passage of U-boats. Daniels and senior American and British officers were sceptical, but Wilson encouraged it, and FDR's persistence, together with a new deep-water mine, brought it about. Never completed, it accounted only for three or four submarines.

Despite his frenetic activity and his reputation as the Navy's organizer of victory, there was a limit to FDR's ability to galvanize the Navy, a self-contained professional institution, and he grew increasingly dissatisfied. Moreover, he sensed that the right place for a Roosevelt and a rising politician was at the front. Repeatedly refused permission to resign but anxious for a war record, he suggested becoming the Navy's European administrator. Rejected again, he begged to inspect naval bases 'over there'. His doggedness was rewarded in July 1918, and he sailed on a three-months' European tour. Crossing on a new destroyer, he was disappointed not to encounter a U-boat, despite several false alarms. He came under sporadic fire at Verdun, but most of his time was occupied in station inspections, skirmishes on naval rivalry with the British, and somewhat ham-fisted (and unauthorized) diplomacy designed to prod Italy into a positive Adriatic strategy. Ultimately, he found his ideal berth, a naval artillery battery on the Western Front, but a month's illness, followed by the Armistice, prevented him donning navy blue. However, public disillusion with America's great crusade ensured that FDR's career suffered little from his lack of a military record. Following the Armistice, he badgered Daniels to send him back to Europe to wind up naval operations, ostensibly in the interests of the Democrats' reputation for efficiency and economy but really to observe the Peace Conference at Paris. Daniels let him go, but only after Roosevelt threatened to disclaim responsibility for any shortcomings in the Navy's war effort. His presence in Europe was unnecessary; Admiral Sims, the theatre commander, reported that he was 'practically confined to looking wise and supervising what is recommended by local commanders and headquarters' (Sims Papers, 24 January 1919, Library of Congress). More significantly, sailing home with the President, he became a firm convert to Wilson's League of Nations.

Between February 1919 and his resignation in August 1920, FDR experienced a clouded finale to his naval career. Trimming the Navy to a peacetime minimum was unexciting, his salary lagged behind massive inflation, and he pondered his political future. Seven successful years in Washington made him a strong candidate for the New York Governorship or US Senate, though he wisely avoided nomination until the omens were favourable. Nevertheless, he staked out an independent position in February 1920 in an address notable for its savage repudiation of Wilson and Daniels. However, when Admiral Sims inspired a partisan Senate investigation of Daniels's wartime administration, FDR's long-term political instinct prompted him to side with his chief rather than the admirals. More seriously, he was implicated in two scandals.

FDR had supported Daniels's endeavours to rehabilitate naval offenders and return them to service, but civilian 'do-gooders' angered naval officers, one of whom accused the administration of returning moral offenders to ships over the objections of commanding officers. FDR became embroiled in a public dispute with this irate officer and had to rely on Daniels to defuse the situation. In the second case, Daniels gave him little help. In a bid to eradicate homosexuality in the naval town of Newport, Rhode Island, Roosevelt had formed a special unit attached to his own office. This had engaged in procurement to trap offenders, and the press exposure indicted Roosevelt for having, at the very least, condoned this conduct. FDR certainly exercised inadequate control over his special section, but it is unlikely that even the cavalier Assistant Secretary lost his political and moral bearings to the extent that he

10

knowingly permitted inadmissible practices, and he put an immediate end to them when they came to his attention. Senate Republicans seized the chance to deal him a perhaps fatal political blow by issuing a partisan report in July 1921 condemning him for negligence, and refusing him an effective right of reply. It was too obviously biased and out of the political season to damage him politically, but it certainly wounded him privately (Morgan, 1985).

Seven years in the Navy Department acquainted Roosevelt with the workings of the Federal Government, honed his administrative skills, brought him a wide range of political, business and labour contacts and established an intimate relationship with the working press. To his acquaintance with his cousin's administration he added a close observation of Woodrow Wilson's, learning much about the scope of executive power and the subtleties of party leadership. By the time he left office, he was developing a more responsible attitude to war and peace and a positive conception of America's global role.

The Darkest Years, 1920–1928

By 1918, the political pendulum was swinging towards conservative Republicanism. Wilson, a figurehead President from October 1919 following a stroke, had antagonized ethnic minorities whose parent countries were disgruntled with the peace, while isolationists were convinced that the League portended perpetual intervention overseas. Farmers were irritated by government regulations, the unions were angered by the government's abandonment of wartime collaboration, and consumers were dismayed by uncontrolled inflation. Democratic leaders, anxious to avoid an administration Presidential nominee in 1920, chose the cheerful, competent, mildly Progressive but staid Ohio Governor, James M. Cox. Unable to jettison Wilsonianism entirely, they nominated for Vice-President a minor official, Franklin D. Roosevelt, as much for his surname as for his record and ability. The Vice-Presidency was an empty office and the Democrats were marked for defeat, but FDR was happy to run. Though none of his biographers adequately explains the crystallization of his Presidential ambitions, it seems to have occurred in 1917, and he was now, in the eyes of himself, Louis Howe and a small but growing number of party leaders, a future Presidential candidate. The Vice-Presidential nomination enabled him to have a

11

'dry run' for the White House, gain national prominence, build a party constituency and stake a claim for the crown when the tide turned the Democrats' way.

Still a moderate Progressive, his thought had developed little since 1912, partly because of his immersion in the Navy and partly because he was unreflective. Intellectual limitations, innate caution, and anxiety not to alienate potential supporters engendered vagueness. He stood for 'a common sense idealism', 'organized progress' and a liberal Democracy. He called for the 'systematized and intensified development of our resources'. Emphasizing governmental rationalization, he favoured a budget office and otherwise pressed for improved education and communications. On Prohibition, cagily, he suggested a referendum. In the campaign, although he toured 32 states and made over a thousand speeches, he remained evasive, trimming to specific audiences.

Cox and Roosevelt were, however, unequivocal spokesmen for Wilson's League. Misjudging the national temper, they believed a vigorous election push could secure Sentate ratification. However, 'In 1920 "normalcy" had a dulcet sound' (Tugwell, 1969, p. 128), and the Republican nominee, Senator Warren Harding, understood the desire for the individualistic pursuit of happiness and an abandonment of 'do-good' Progressivism at home and abroad. Nevertheless, Roosevelt acted as if heading for victory, at full throttle – the flashing smile, hearty laugh, purposeful stride, stern countenance at the lectern, light tenor voice – and his performance reflected a 'conscious development of the Roosevelt identity' (Tugwell, 1969, p. 126). The campaign confirmed his equable temperament and remarkable ability to absorb and utilize political knowledge, and demonstrated his extraordinary rapport with audiences and the press. However, little that he said or did could prevent a resounding defeat.

From November 1920 to November 1928, Roosevelt was in the political wilderness, adroitly sidestepping invitations to run for the Senate or the Governorship. However, he was never more active in Democratic counsels, though little of his advice was taken. The party was rent on every issue. 'Wet' anti-Prohibitionists fought 'Dry' supporters. Wilsonian internationalists clashed with rock-ribbed isolationists. Progressives contended with conservatives. Rural Westerners and Southerners disliked the urban East. Many from the West and South belonged to the racist, paranoid Ku Klux Klan, then at its apogee; Eastern, immigrant, Catholic, Jewish and liberal forces abhorred it. Even the tariff now divided Democrats, many swinging away from the party's historic low-tariff stance. FDR, always sensitive to the need to maximize support, presented himself as the party healer. It required him to be relatively un-committed and slightly devious. Supported by the untiring and selfless Howe, he tried hard to discover grounds for unity, to fashion a permanent businesslike organization, and to promote the party. In particular, he saw the potential of female suffrage (granted in 1920) and helped to organize a women's section.

Outside politics, FDR practised law, though chiefly for political contacts. He lacked the patient, detached personality to be a happy or notable lawyer. A vigorous and relatively successful vice-president of a bond company, he dabbled also in a few eccentric ventures and fluttered mildly on the stock market, losing about as much as he made. Otherwise, he busied himself in philanthropy and planted trees at Hyde Park.

This idyll was shattered by a polio attack whilst on holiday in August 1921 which permanently paralysed his legs. The effect of the virus was aggravated by an icy ducking, followed by fighting a forest fire, but FDR was also physically and mentally drained; a succession of blows may have disturbed his normal equanimity (Morgan, 1985). Apart from the naval offenders' and Newport scandals, a wartime relationship with a society belle almost brought about a divorce. The marriage, which, because of Roosevelt's relative self-centredness, had never truly blossomed, survived as a partnership. When the polio struck, however, Eleanor's devotion was unquestioned and, with Howe, she rescued Franklin from despair and sustained his political ambition, becoming herself a significant politician. Roosevelt, convinced he would walk again, sampled several agonizing but unavailing treatments, culminating in his purchase and rehabilitation of a rundown Georgia spa, Warm Springs, relaxing his wasted legs in its warm pool and acquainting himself with Southern politics and backwardness. Confined mostly to a wheelchair, he could walk only a few excruciating steps encased in heavy steel braces.

Polio hastened his slow maturation. He became more patient and sympathetic, focused more exclusively on politics, and read widely though eclectically; there is little evidence that he became more reflective or intellectually consistent. His illness reinforced his remarkable self-control, serenity, courage and sense of humour – he joked about his affliction to put others at their ease. He returned

2 The Road to the White House (1928–1933)

The Governorship of New York, 1928–1932

Between 1924 and 1928, Roosevelt recuperated at Warm Springs and avoided nomination for office. At the 1928 Democratic convention, he successfully nominated Al Smith for President. A four-term progressive Governor of New York, Smith was easily the nation's leading Democrat but, despite Smith's drift towards business conservatism, the nation regarded the Republican Herbert Hoover as the better guarantor of continued prosperity. Moreover Smith was a Catholic, a Wet, and of urban, immigrant background; rural, Protestant, old-stock Americans were prejudiced against him. Doubtful about Smith's prospects, Democratic leaders wanted Roosevelt for Governor to help pull Smith through in upstate New York. FDR, pleading the need for more work on his legs, demurred; unspoken was his conviction that he would be dragged down in Smith's impending débâcle. Three successive electoral defeats would label him a permanent loser. An adamant state party drafted him; a refusal to run might have cost him party support in more auspicious times.

Though never Smith's political intimate, Roosevelt campaigned loyally for him. His characteristically vigorous campaign in 1928 proved his physical fitness; his new fact-finder and speech draftsman, Sam Rosenman, noted that 'his disability had no effect upon his energy' (Rosenman, 1952, p. 48). Frances Perkins (1947, p. 39) watched him carried to a meeting over a fire escape:

> Those of us who saw this incident ... realized this man had accepted the ultimate humility of being helped physically. He had accepted it smiling... He got up on his braces, adjusted

them, straightened himself, smoothed his hair, linked his arm in his son Jim's, and walked out onto the platform as if this were nothing unusual.

The genial Roosevelt campaigned on Smith's great progressive record, which he fully endorsed. Though Smith lost his state and the Presidency, FDR was surprisingly elected Governor by a few thousand votes. It represented a turning point in Democratic politics. The provincial Smith, now backsliding from progressivism, was yesterday's man. New York, a powerful, populous state, so heterogenous as to be the nation in microcosm, was a launching pad for the 1932 nomination. Roosevelt could be tomorrow's leader – provided he could be re-elected to the Governorship in 1930 by a comfortable margin.

Entering office in January 1929, Roosevelt inherited a well-oiled administration. Smith, in a political limbo and sceptical of FDR's capacity, hoped to be his successor's puppeteer. Roosevelt, with one eye on the White House, was determined to be his own man; thus began a rapid deterioration in his relations with Smith. He expanded Smith's progressivism – notably aid to farmers, pensions, industrial welfare, a war on crime, conservation and publicly produced hydroelectric power. Conservative Republicans, dominant in the legislature, robotically opposed any liberal bills. FDR, already a pastmaster in broadcasting (Freidel, 1954), seized the initiative, outwitted the Republicans and forced them to give way on most of his measures by the summer of 1930. Rebuilding the Democratic party in the rural areas, he undermined the Republicans' appeal in their heartland. He displayed his vigour and concern by inspecting all parts of the state. What he could not see himself, he learned from interrogating others. 'Roosevelt could "get" a problem infinitely better when he had a vicarious experience through a vivid description of a typical case,' wrote Frances Perkins (1947, p. 80), his Industrial Commissioner. 'His vivid imagination and sympathy helped him to "see" from a word picture.' Well before the vote in November 1930, his re-election was assured, and he polled a record majority.

Much of FDR's effectiveness derived from the loyal and efficient team he assembled, most of whom continued to serve him during his Presidency. The sardonic, suspicious Howe was still chief-of-staff. 'He had only one loyalty in life – and it was a kind of religion – Franklin D. Roosevelt... His chief ambition was to be the

16

manager of this President-making campaign' (Rosenman, 1952, pp. 37–8). A Columbia University political scientist, Raymond Moley, advised on the administration of justice. A fellow 'gentleman farmer' from Dutchess County, Henry Morgenthau Jr., worked on agriculture. Felix Frankfurter, a Harvard law professor, helped on power and business matters. Political management was in the hands of the 'suave, astute, knowledgeable' Edward J. Flynn, boss of the Bronx (Davis, 1985, p. 32) and Jim Farley, the big, genial, painstaking state party chairman. Eleanor Roosevelt, though busy with her own furniture workshop and school teaching, carried out numerous inspections for her husband and brought him intellectual, labour and social work contacts; theirs had become a 'symbiotic' relationship (Davis, 1985, p. 118). 'It was easy to work with him,' Rosenman (1952, p. 36) recalled, and this inner circle, marvelling at his courage, ability to grasp salient points quickly, his political acumen, indefatigable good humour and superabundant energy, gave freely of its abilities and time. FDR, at home in an executive role, carried the Governorship with dignity and élan (Tugwell, 1969). His sweeping re-election made him the Democratic front runner for 1932, but another, greater hurdle arose.

FDR had long maintained that laissez-faire Republicanism would engender depression; the electoral tide would then run for the Democrats. Vague as to the causes and timing of the catastrophe, FDR, like most Americans, was surprised by the Wall Street stock market crash in October 1929, and he was not fully aware of the seriousness and persistence of the collapse until January 1931, when Frances Perkins showed him unemployment figures (one million in New York; seven million in the nation). Apart from reducing tax burdens on the long-depressed farmers, FDR was slow to act until it was clear by the summer of 1931 that the depression was still deepening, no solutions were in sight, and customary emergency funds were drying up. Electoral calculations apart, FDR was incapable of continued inaction; he was not prepared to see people homeless and starving. 'In Roosevelt, the practical politician and the humanitarian statesman worked together' (Rosenman, 1952, p. 41). Already pursuing pensions and unemployment insurance as long-term anti-poverty measures, in August 1931 he set up a Temporary Emergency Relief Administration, employing the jobless on public works and funded by a $20 million tax increase (thus avoiding a morale-sapping dole, an unbalanced budget and borrowing; FDR was almost as orthodox fiscally as Hoover). TERA represented the novel conviction that the State should care 'for those of its citizens who find themselves victims of such adverse circumstances' through no fault of their own (FDR in Rosenman, 1952, p. 59). A gaunt, lanky social worker, Harry Hopkins, ran TERA with zest and efficiency and went on to head New Deal relief agencies. Though subsequent loan injections could not hide the fact that the crisis was far too extensive for state resources, nevertheless TERA at once made FDR the nation's leading combatant against the Great Depression. It revealed also his willingness to break the mould of conventional wisdom in his search for remedies for an unprecedented situation.

Leading from the Front: the First Presidential Campaign, 1932

Despite FDR's absorption in gubernatorial duties, 'he was also a candidate for president every moment of that service' (Tugwell, 1969, p. 147). He denied interest, but his managers foraged for party support. Throwing his hat into the ring in January 1932, he had to demonstrate his fitness to the nation. Since the Republican failure to cure the Depression virtually guaranteed a Democratic victory, Roosevelt faced several rivals. Even if they could be seen off in party primary elections, state party caucuses or the national party convention, many Democrats considered him an arrogant light-weight, and a 'Stop Roosevelt' bloc was likely. Conservative opponents, controlling the party machinery, tried on several occasions to trip him up. FDR could hardly avoid being the front runner although he knew he might run out of steam or funds and present later candidates with a ready-made target. He resolved to secure the necessary two-thirds of the delegates before the convention opened. Farley opened a headquarters in New York in the spring of 1931 and in the summer criss-crossed the nation 'as a sort of combination political drummer and listening post' (Farley, 1948, p. 12), sounding out state leaders on a Roosevelt candidacy; optimistically, he predicted victory on the first convention ballot.

Farley's rashness betrayed his inexperience in national politics. At the Chicago convention in June 1932, FDR held a commanding lead but lay a hundred votes short of the two-thirds majority required; moreover, some delegates wavered. Farley, 'glad-handing every delegate and leader I could reach', ran the floor show. On the first ballot, 'I was so sure that the opposition lines would break... Nothing happened. Not a single delegate shifted' (1948, p. 21).

After three inconclusive ballots, Roosevelt faced disaster. Farley's frantic negotiations centred on the Texas and California delegations pledged to the Speaker of the House of Representatives, John Garner. Fortunately Garner, a staunch party regular, chiefly interested in preventing deadlock, brusquely released his delegates. Rewarded with the Vice-Presidential nomination, Garner termed it characteristically as 'not worth a quart of warm spit'. FDR had cleared the two-thirds hurdle at the eleventh hour.

Roosevelt needed to flesh out his vague liberalism and focus on national problems. Business and legal advisers being intellectually bankrupt, FDR, who had noted Moley's facility with words and ideas, looked to the universities for new perspectives on the Depression. By April 1932, an informal 'Brains Trust' headed by Moley included 'Doc' O'Connor (FDR's law partner), Rosenman and two of Moley's Columbia colleagues, Rex Tugwell, an agricultural economist, and Adolf Berle, an expert on 'credit and corporations' (Moley, 1939, p. 18; Rosenman, 1952). FDR had 'an exceptionally agile mind' which was put through 'a rigorous Brains Trust course in socio-economics' (Tugwell, 1969, pp. 215–16). Many people were subjected to FDR's 'intellectual ransacking' out of which 'his own thinking was brought into sharper focus' (Moley, 1939, p. 20; Rosenman, 1952, p. 70). The Brains Trust shaped a nationalistic, holistic, collectivist economic policy based on three premises: it believed that 'our ills were domestic ... the remedies would have to be internal'; it recognized 'the need not only for an extension of the government's regulatory power to prevent abuses ... but for ... controls to stimulate and stabilize economic activity'; and it felt that 'any attempt to atomize big business must destroy America's greatest contribution to a higher standard of living for the body of its citizenry – the development of mass production' (Moley, 1939, p. 24).

The Brains Trusters drafted speeches based on FDR's general intentions, and the candidate worked them over. Most of his major statements in 1932 reflected Brains Trust advice, but he was never the prisoner of any group, partly because he lacked intellectual consistency but largely because of 'the persistence of political criteria in all he did' (Tugwell, 1969, p. 151). Roosevelt was 'a total politician' (Jesse Jones, quoted in Romasco, 1983, p. 4), and policy served political needs.

The first Roosevelt–Moley collaboration, a brief party political broadcast (April 1932, Roosevelt Papers, 1928–32, pp. 624–7), spoke for 'the forgotten man at the bottom of the economic pyramid' in contrast to the Hoover administration 'which can think in terms only of the top of the social and economic structure'. Emphasizing what was to be his most consistent theme, the interdependence of the agricultural and industrial communities, FDR pointed out the need to restore the purchasing power of the agricultural half of the population, to relieve the mortgage anxieties of homeowners and farmers, and to negotiate reciprocal trade agreements. Reflecting advanced economic thought, he asserted that the Great Depression was a crisis of abundance, the central issue being the just and efficient distribution of America's cornucopia. Acknowledging 'that we are in the midst of an emergency at least equal to war', he urged a total mobilization of resources equal to the wartime effort of 1917–18; 'the analogue of war' (Leuchtenburg, in Braeman, 1964, p. 81) recurred in the early New Deal. At Oglethorpe University, Georgia (May 1932), in 'the sincerest, most unpolitical statement of his real attitudes and convictions' (Tugwell, 1969, p. 219), FDR spoke of 'adequate planning' and declared that 'the country demands bold, persistent experimentation. It is commonsense to take a method and try it; if it fails, admit it frankly and try another. But above all try something' (Roosevelt Papers, 1928–32, pp. 639–47). A commitment to government activism, the address was an acknowledgement that no universally agreed or tested cure for the Depression existed.

In a characteristic headline-stealing gesture, FDR flew from Albany to Chicago to accept the nomination (2 July). Identifying the Democratic party as 'the bearer of Liberalism and of progress', he declared 'this is no time for fear, for reaction or for timidity.' Attacking Republican fatalism and inaction, he argued that 'economic laws are not made by nature. They are made by human beings' and thus could be rewritten to meet changing conditions. Promising that his administration 'will assume bold leadership in distress relief', he listed his objectives: economical administration; a self-financing public works programme; a shorter working week; the repeal of Prohibition; a 'truth-in-securities' act to regulate speculation; 'a definite land policy', including employment of the young jobless on conservation projects; a price support programme for farmers involving planned production; and 'work and security' for all. Concluding 'I pledge you, I pledge myself to a new deal for the American people,' he unwittingly gave his Presidency its indelible title (Roosevelt Papers, 1928–32, pp. 647–59).

Following the convention, Roosevelt demonstrated his fitness on a cruise, and mended fences with Smith and other opponents. A breezy, brilliant but erratic ex-soldier and businessman, Hugh Johnson, joined the Brains Trust, which was further diluted by party elders. Many hands contributed to the campaign addresses, which became blander as Roosevelt sought to unify the nation and avoid alienating potential supporters (Tugwell, 1968, 1969). The election was won three months before polling day, Hoover's fate being sealed by the brutal eviction of Great War veterans from their Washington 'Hooverville' (shanty town) on his orders. There was no need for FDR to barnstorm, but 'campaigning, for him, was unadulterated joy' (Moley, 1939, p. 52). 'He enjoyed the freedom and getting out among the people ... His personal relationship with the crowds was on a warm, simple level of a friendly, neighbourly exchange of affection' (Perkins, 1947, p. 91). Covering thirty-two states and 13,000 miles in eight weeks, FDR made sixteen major and sixty-seven minor addresses and numerous 'back platform' extemporaneous remarks. Moley noted that 'he never wearied or lost his good humor' and 'never stopped having a wonderful time' (1939, p. 52). Although Hoover attacked him, FDR refused to answer the President; speeches changed few votes. Freidel (1956) believes there were few differences between them, but Rosen (1977) claims the gulf was considerable. Apart from striking personal contrasts – Hoover, lips turned down, weary, prosaic; Roosevelt, buoyant, 'smiles and smiles and smiles' – one cannot envisage Hoover espousing public power production, conservation camps, agricultural production controls and especially Federal relief payments. By October, 'It was more like a triumphal tour than a campaign for Roosevelt' (Rosenman, 1952, p. 89). The election in November, however, represented a decisive rejection of Hoover rather than a mandate for Roosevelt. Nevertheless, gaining 22.8 million votes to Hoover's 15.75 million and winning forty-two of the forty-eight states, FDR carried in 'on his coat tails' substantial Democratic majorities in both Houses of Congress.

The Winter of Waiting and Wasting, 1932–1933

The four months between the election (6 November) and the inauguration (4 March) proved almost fatal. Hoover and the 'lame duck' Congress were demoralized, divided and drained. The economy slid deeper into the mire. Thirteen to seventeen million were unemployed, as many again on reduced incomes, and the rest insecure. Farmers were being forced off their lands; hundreds of thousands lost their homes; policemen and teachers went unpaid as even the largest cities approached bankruptcy. Two million vagrants roamed the country. Soup kitchen queues lengthened daily, and local relief, public and philanthropic, never adequate, dried up. Hundreds starved; thousands scavenged the city dumps, where others lived in packing-case 'Hoovervilles'. In February, the banking structure, long a weak link (too many small units and irresponsible speculation with depositors' money), cracked; by inauguration day, many banks were insolvent and many more were shaky. Communists and Socialists believed that capitalism was in its death throes. Yet, as FDR observed, 'Wild radicalism has made few converts, and the greatest tribute I can pay to my countrymen is that in these days of crushing want there persists an orderly and hopeful spirit' (Roosevelt Papers, 1928–32, p. 649). There were disturbances – depositors battered bank doors, farmers resisted foreclosures and ditched surplus produce; but, remarkably, popular faith in democracy, capitalism and 'the American dream' remained, though no one knew for how long. For the moment, bewilderment, numbness and lingering hope held sway.

During the winter, Hoover, convinced that world forces were responsible for the Depression, sought FDR's adherence to internationalist economic measures. 'Roosevelt's cardinal object was to keep clear of the wrecked Hoover administration' (Burns, 1956, p. 145) and, though tempted by the internationalist view and obliged politically to talk to Hoover, he remained loyal to the Brains Trust's economic nationalism (Moley, 1939; Rosen, 1977). In the meantime, he formed his 'cabinet' (which had no constitutional or political standing). Moley (1939, p. 111) termed it 'a rather savorless cabinet pudding' and the only obvious principle was 'For Roosevelt Before Chicago'. Four of the ten merit attention. Henry Wallace, Secretary of Agriculture, a dabbler in mysticism, was highly respected in the farming world. 'Honest Harold' Ickes, Secretary of the Interior (a 'Department of the Environment' – and much else), a crusty but able prima donna, was a Republican progressive. Jim Farley, the organizer of victory and national party chairman, became Postmaster-General, the dispenser of patronage. The most interesting appointment was Frances Perkins as Secretary of Labor (normally a union leader's plum). The first woman cabinet member, her appointment was a tribute to her ability and FDR's shrewd realization that women constituted over half the electorate.

Three weeks before the inauguration, FDR narrowly missed assassination in Miami. Unhurt, he was a study in calmness, courage and concern for others; the troubled nation warmed to the President-elect's steadfastness.

22

3 The New Deal (1933–1945)

The First Hundred Days, March to June 1933

The bleak Inauguration Day (4 March 1933) weather reflected the nation's mood. No incoming President save Lincoln had faced so dismal a prospect. The national income was under half the 1929 figure, debts were colossal, almost eighteen million were jobless, and economic indicators continued to plunge.

In an inaugural address touching greatness in its eloquence, spirit and assured delivery (Roosevelt Papers, 1933, pp. 11–16), Roosevelt sketched relief, recovery and reform measures, but the speech's significance lay in its psychology. Invoking biblical and military imagery he declared that 'the only thing we have to fear is fear itself' and expressed confidence in the capacity of the nation, its institutions and himself to defeat the depression without radical change. Promising 'action, and action now' to restore domestic prosperity, he gave scant attention to world problems. Castigating the 'money changers' as the perpetrators of the distress, he identified an equitable distribution of the nation's undoubted abundance as a fundamental necessity. Employing the 'analogue of war', he pictured 'a trained and loyal army willing to sacrifice for the good of a common discipline', drawing his loudest applause for his willingness to exercise 'broad Executive power' to fight the depression (Freidel, 1973; Schlesinger, 1959). FDR held that democracies perished not from boldness but from timidity. A half-million laudatory messages testified to the public's approbation. This accord was strengthened four days later at a press conference. Roosevelt, 'a picture of ease and confidence' (Davis, 1986, p. 35), engendered a bantering, informal spirit, but there was no doubt who was in command.

A day later, Congress met and passed, almost sight unseen, an

Emergency Banking Act authorizing the reopening of sound banks and shoring up others. Roosevelt eschewed reform, drawing criticism (Bernstein, 1970) for failing to nationalize the prostrate banks, but radical proposals would have invited wrangles, prolonging national paralysis and delaying other vital measures; the 'money changers' would feel the regulatory lash when the crisis was less acute. Roosevelt strengthened his rapport with the people in the first 'Fireside Chat' on 12 March. Explaining the bank crisis and the steps taken to overcome it, this radio address was so simple that 'even the bankers understood it' (Schlesinger, 1959, p. 13). A polished broadcaster, FDR imagined himself seated across the fireside in every parlour (Perkins, 1947). Broadcasts afforded him a platform for major policy statements, and none save Churchill exhibited such a mastery over the airwaves. In this chat (Roosevelt Papers, 1933, pp. 61–5), Roosevelt affirmed that there was 'nothing complex or radical' in the bank act, and exhorted: 'You people must have faith, you must not be stampeded by rumors or guesses. Let us unite in banishing fear ... It is your problem no less than it is mine. Together we cannot fail.' Hoover had said much the same, unavailingly, but Roosevelt's warm, authoritative tone established 'a real dialogue between Franklin and the people' (Eleanor Roosevelt, in Leuchtenburg, 1963, p. 331). The next day, money flowed back into the banks.

Roosevelt contemplated no further urgent measures, but advisers pressed him to capitalize on Congress's willingness to act. The early New Deal, however, dealt old cards, out-Hoovering Hoover in budget pruning. Roosevelt, whose 'fiscal notions were wholly orthodox' (Schlesinger, 1959, p. 10), shared widespread fears of runaway inflation and national bankruptcy. He slashed Federal salaries and defence spending, cut ex-soldiers' pensions and refused to advance their bonus due in 1945. Many Democrats, proponents of Federal relief spending and fearful of the veterans' lobby, balked at these economies. Roosevelt brandished the party loyalty stick, dangled the patronage carrot, and sweetened the nasty medicine by legalizing beer, the first step in the repeal of Prohibition (accomplished in December 1933). A second Bonus Expeditionary Force found him as unwilling to pay the bonus as Hoover but Roosevelt lost neither his nerve nor his compassion. Music, coffee and relief work dispersed the ex-soldiers. 'Hoover sent the Army, Roosevelt sent his wife,' commented one veteran (Schlesinger, 1959, p. 15).

Roosevelt appreciated that the early New Deal had been thoroughly negative. Distinguishing disingenuously between a 'regular' budget, which he hoped to balance, and an 'emergency' relief budget, Roosevelt sought to make recovery programmes self-financing – establishing revolving funds, instituting loans rather than grants, and thriftily killing two birds with one stone. A classic example of this last device was the Civilian Conservation Corps, a 'stunning idea' largely inspired by Roosevelt (Moley, 1939, p. 173). FDR characteristically 'conceived the project, boldly rushed it through and happily left it to others to worry about details' (Perkins, 1947, p. 144). Combining the improvement of the national estate, 'national service' for the young and unemployment relief, the CCC gave unemployed city youth a taste of country life and promoted conservation. 'Perhaps no law passed during the Hundred Days expressed more passionately a central presidential concern' than the Tennessee Valley Act (Schlesinger, 1959, p. 319). Flowing through seven south-eastern states, the unruly Tennessee flooded them, leached topsoil from denuded hillsides and inhibited navigation. Chronically poor for a century, the region's three million people were bereft of modern services, communications, education and economic opportunity. Yet the river abounded in hydroelectric power sites, and Roosevelt proposed a public power network for a region where scarcely anyone turned a switch. Producing its own power would give the Government a 'yardstick' by which to judge private electricity rates; a Federal fertilizer plant would enable a yardstick to be applied to private top-dressing prices. Roosevelt further envisaged a comprehensive regional plan embracing navigation, flood control, reforestation, improved communications, preventive health care, educational opportunities and economic diversification, carried out by 'a corporation clothed with the power of Government but possessed of the flexibility and initiative of a private enterprise' (Roosevelt Papers, 1933, p. 122). A Republican described TVA, not without a grain of truth, as 'patterned closely after one of the soviet dreams' (Schlesinger, 1959, p. 326).

Farming had been depressed since 1920, and FDR constantly stressed the 'interdependence' of agriculture and industry. Farmers' purchasing power must be restored to enable them to buy industrial products. FDR was attracted to 'domestic allotment', by which farmers would agree to crop limitation in return for a subsidy derived from a tax on agricultural processors. However, in the interests of speed and flexibility, he accepted an omnibus act embracing all the possibilities and setting up an Agricultural Adjustment Administration (AAA). A Farm Credit Administration rationalized Federal farm loan schemes and refinanced farmers' mortgages. From October 1933, surplus farm produce was distributed to the urban poor via a Federal Surplus Relief Corporation, while a Commodity Credit Corporation lent money to farmers who took land out of cultivation.

In the cities, a Home Owners' Loan Corporation refinanced mortgages, and FDR was persuaded by his relief director from New York days, Harry Hopkins, to set up a Federal Emergency Relief Administration, disbursing initially $500 million, divided evenly between matching grants to the states and discretionary payments to the worst-hit areas. The institution of FERA at a time when unemployment was estimated at 17.9 million, 75 per cent of whom were in actual distress (Perkins, 1947), marked the acceptance of Federal responsibility for the well-being of all citizens and heralded the advent of the American welfare state. FERA paid a dole, but FDR and Hopkins disliked doles as unproductive and morale-sapping. However, Roosevelt was also sceptical about the alternative, an extensive public works programme. He doubted the need for many new facilities, feared business complaints of competition, and believed it would prevent a balanced budget. Nevertheless, Hopkins, Perkins and Congressional progressives cajoled him into an unprecedented public works appropriation of $3.3 billion (the progressives had urged $5 billion; FDR proposed $1 billion). However, Roosevelt cannily ensured that many projects would be ultimately self-financing and that some normal expenditures would be met out of the programme's funds (naval rearmament, for example).

Financial security was underpinned by the 'Truth-in-Securities' Act, regulating the investment market in the interests of investors by curbing 'insider trading' among other things, and by the Glass–Steagall Act, which separated merchant banking from ordinary deposit banking and included Federal insurance of deposits. FDR opposed deposit insurance as impractical, expensive and likely to drag down sound banks, but Congress, never a rubber stamp, insisted, and the scheme enjoyed outstanding success. Like the FCA, HOLC and Commodity Credit Corporation, the Federal Deposit Insurance Corporation was underwritten by the Reconstruction Finance Corporation. A Hoover agency intended to prop up big business, it was transformed under FDR into the world's largest bank, lending $10.5 billion and serving farmers, small investors and small businesses.

Business had declined by almost two-thirds and manufacturing production by a half since 1929. Businessmen suggested government–business co-operative recovery programmes, but Roosevelt decided these were too vague for early action (Davis, 1986). Once again, Congress forced his hand with a thirty-hour week bill to spread employment and maintain wage levels. Roosevelt regarded it as too rigid, too limited, and probably unconstitutional, but it seemed likely to pass. Intent on retaining the political initiative, he authorized at least two groups to draw up alternative proposals, airily commanding them to compromise their differences. The resulting National Industrial Recovery Act envisaged a partnership between government, business, labour and consumers based on codes of fair competition which limited hours, established reasonable wages, abolished child labour and fixed production and prices (the anti-trust laws having been suspended). A step towards the corporate state, the National Recovery Administration was descended from the War Industries Board of 1917–19 and the advanced academic and business thought of the past decade, including the Brains Trusters. Labour's friends insisted on basic organizing rights, which were granted in Section 7a. The public works programme was part of the same act, its sponsors believing that relief projects would stimulate the economy if they were dovetailed with NRA. The act, which had something for almost everyone, was 'essentially an expression of the broker state' (Burns, 1956, p. 192), and Roosevelt described it as 'a challenge to industry which has long insisted that, given the right to act in unison, it could do much for the general good which has hitherto been unlawful' (Roosevelt Papers, 1933, p. 252).

It was then mid-June, and the weary Congress dispersed. In his first hundred days, FDR had made ten major speeches, issued fifteen important messages, signed fifteen epochal statutes and received the world's leaders. It was, recalled Moley (1939, p. 191), 'a record of sheer effort ... that has no parallel in the history of American Presidents'. A mediocre candidate metamorphosed overnight into a second Lincoln, giving a beaten nation the decisive leadership and self-confidence that it craved. Though he bent to pressures from advisers, lobbies and Congress, Roosevelt managed always to retain the political initiative. Though always alert to political considerations and endeavouring to maintain a nationwide

27

coalition, FDR was receptive to any practical idea for waging war on the depression; intellectual inconsistency troubled him little. Moley (1939, p. 128) observed, 'As the weeks ran on in March, the city of Washington became a mecca for ... goo-goos of all types, who at last perceived that a new political era was at hand and who took it to be a kind of crusade which the discontented of every variety were invited to join.' Anne McCormick (in Freidel, 1964, p. 4) reported, 'You feel the stir of movement, of adventure, even of elation. You never saw before in Washington so much government, or so much animation in government ... for the first time the capital feels like the center of the country.' The nearest parallel was with World War I. 'Official Washington,' noted Moley (1939, p. 191), 'was in the grip of a war psychology as surely as it had been in 1917.' Roosevelt, 'who'd found a happy way of life' (Moley, 1939, p. 191), appeared unaffected by the turmoil. 'Considering the boiling disturbances all round the New Deal periphery,' commented Tugwell (1969, p. 294), 'the center at the White House was remarkably tranquil and easy.' The President's command seemed both total and effortless.

The New Deal in Action, 1933–1935

Most ideological creeds had a stake in the New Deal, none dominated it, and Roosevelt aimed at amelioration, not revolution. The New Deal ranged untidily from conservative budget cutting, through corporatism in business, agrarian populism, sharp curbs on the money changers and token relief for the jobless, to socialism in the Tennessee Valley. 'Not a plan with form and content' (Perkins, 1947, p. 135), unsurprisingly the New Deal enjoyed mixed results. Farmers' varied experiences were typical. By 1936, the AAA, assisted in crop reduction by vast dust storms, had raised farm income by 50 per cent from the 1932 level, while the FCA refinanced a fifth of farm mortgages and cut farmers' debts by a billion dollars. The AAA earned its spurs by rushing aid to the farmers in the wake of natural catastrophes, and agriculture now enjoyed a permanent relationship with government. Though thousands of farmers (especially in the South) were forced to quit, many more would have lost their land but for the AAA (Badger, 1982). Kirkendall (in Braeman, 1975) described the farm programmes as the greatest success of New Deal collectivism, yet they also manifested serious shortcomings. The AAA benefited chiefly the larger farmers, who dominated the local production control committees, and accelerated the shift to larger 'factory farming' units, though it otherwise effected no radical changes (Badger, 1982). Minor crops received little or no assistance. The rise in farm income did little to boost general economic recovery, for farmers were hoarders rather than spenders, while the processing tax raised food prices. The food industry lobby curtailed distribution of surplus produce to the destitute. Romasco (1983) criticized Roosevelt for giving agriculture priority over the larger industrial sector. However, a third of the American people depended upon agriculture, and FDR meant to retain the farm vote; political realism dovetailed with economic logic.

The industrial recovery programme, the National Recovery Administration, was headed by the Brains Truster Hugh Johnson, who 'saw all life as a melodrama slightly streaked with farce' (Schlesinger, 1959, p. 105). His dynamism and flair for publicity were initial assets, climaxing in a national victory drive (summer 1933) reminiscent of the Great War, symbolized by the 'Blue Eagle', as management, labour and the public mobilized under banners, parades and songs to put millions back to work, establish fair prices, minimum wages and maximum hours, and abolish sweatshops and child labour. Employment rose by two million and purchasing power by three billion dollars, raising extravagant hopes that the depression was on the run. The crusade faded in the autumn despite Johnson's ballyhoo, and NRA steadily lost popularity and effectiveness. The act itself was constitutionally suspect, and Johnson never dared use the draconian power to license business, depending instead on publicity, moral pressure and cajolery. The codes of fair competition were drawn up almost entirely by business trade associations to satisfy their immediate needs. Consumers received no more than a cursory nod, while labour complained that Section 7a was being widely ignored. There were too many codes, resulting in pettifogging bureaucracy; they should have been confined to the handful of major industries. Small businessmen undoubtedly found it difficult to meet code standards, and business as a whole, once the springtime paralysis was over, began to chafe against the NRA harness. The opportunity to plan industry's future was not seized (Tugwell, 1969), and initial gains in employment, wages and prices were not always sustained. The public works provision of the act was divorced from industrial recovery, the two proceeding at different paces with no mutual benefits. Roosevelt felt that together they were beyond one person's capacity. Johnson's erratic personal life and chaotic administration ultimately proved so embarrassing that Roosevelt (who was chronically incapable of sacking anyone) finally eased him out in September 1934. Roosevelt's interest waxed and waned, and he never committed himself fully to the holistic policy of co-operating with business, but retained a strong attachment to the atomistic philosophy of 'trust-busting' (breaking up the great combines). The NRA may have slowed recovery but it curbed sweating and child labour, introduced the concepts of consumers' rights, minimum wages and maximum hours, and legitimized trade union activity; most of these gains were made permanent by subsequent legislation. Moreover, government gained experience in economic mobilization which proved invaluable in World War II (Schlesinger, 1959).

Johnson had envisaged a quick-acting public works programme priming the industrial pump, but the Public Works Administration was slow to get under way. The responsibility for tardiness has been laid upon the Administrator, Secretary of the Interior 'Honest Harold' Ickes (e.g., Moley, 1939), who scrutinized minutely every project. In fact, Ickes quickly allocated almost all of the $3.3 billion. Implementation was delayed by the lengthy preparations required for the major dam, navigation, highway, airport, railroad, hospital and rearmament programmes undertaken. Moreover, heavyweight public works were capital-intensive rather than labour-intensive. Nevertheless, the PWA, ultimately spending over $6 billion, was responsible for a third of the country's hospitals, slum clearances, thousands of schools and other substantial improvements to the nation's infrastructure; it was also honest and efficient, and in time absorbed surplus labour and stimulated the construction and heavy engineering industries. Nevertheless, as the winter of 1933–4 cast its cold shadow, Roosevelt and Hopkins recognized the political and humanitarian necessity for instant public works. In a blitzkrieg mobilization of four million people in thirty days, Hopkins's Civil Works Administration, commandeering FERA staff, lavished $2 billion on roads, 40,000 schools, 1,000 airports, and the support of artists, musicians, writers, archaeologists and teachers. The hard core unemployed were supported through the winter, and the CWA enlivened, entertained and educated America. It was not, however, a plan for all seasons. Critics lambasted some make-work schemes as 'boondoggling', and FDR, alarmed by the cost and the prospect of a permanent class of reliefers, terminated CWA at the first breath of spring.

On a more modest scale, relief continued via the Civilian Conservation Corps, which took 250,000 unemployed youths from the cities for several months of tree planting, soil conservation and other environmental improvement work. In ten years, three million young men from all corners of the nation gained fitness, self-confidence, self-reliance and pride in their accomplishments. The CCC was an almost unalloyed success, though a later generation would criticize the segregation of blacks and the absence of women. The TVA was also quickly underway; within eighteen months it was generating cheap power, preventing floods, expanding navigation and tourism, and educating farmers in new techniques. Though it never quite fulfilled Roosevelt's comprehensive dream of regional planning, it transformed the lives of three million forgotten men and women, most spectacularly through the almost universal electrification of the great valley. Before TVA, one farm in ten had power; within twenty years it was nine in ten, the work being accomplished mainly by farmers' co-operatives under the Rural Electrification Administration, funded by the RFC and enjoying FDR's close support (Davis, 1986). Managerial dissension, bruising legal encounters with private power, the inertia of local vested interests, the scars of segregation and the faltering local response to 'grass roots' democracy inhibited total success. Nevertheless, it represented a spectacular triumph for FDR's vision, a model for other nations and, he hoped (in vain), for other great valleys in the USA.

One fifth of suburban homes were saved by HOLC, but it also foreclosed on 100,000 unemployed people (Leuchtenburg, 1963). The Federal Deposit Insurance Corporation, a good fairy to small depositors, waved its magic wand over the banks, too; even in good times, banks had failed almost daily; now, fatalities became rare. The Truth-in-Securities Act was given real teeth by the Securities and Exchange Commission in 1934, a watchdog on Wall Street and the small investor's friend. The Reciprocal Trade Agreements Act (1934), a characteristic Roosevelt hybrid, blended the Republican high-tariff tradition with the Democratic low-tariff creed. While the general tariff remained sky-high, bilateral agreements undercut it, though trade benefited little.

The New Deal was frankly domestic and FDR only flirted with economic internationalism. Foreign leaders trooped to Washington in the spring of 1933 for talks on debts, currency stabilization, tariffs and the gold standard. Roosevelt was pleasant but noncommittal. He had been committed to the London Economic Conference (summer 1933) by Hoover, but his approach was casual in the extreme; he seems to have understood little and cared less about it. His delegation was incompatible and incompetent. After a month of vacillation, the President effectively torpedoed the conference by blandly announcing America's intention to retain its freedom of action to put its own house in order. FDR has been accused of perpetuating world depression and thus contributing to the Second World War, but no country was willing to make concessions, and most had acted to save their own skins. There was little chance of success in London, but FDR's indifference, incomprehension and indecisiveness earned the United States a reputation for perfidy. Unconcerned, Roosevelt enacted a daily farce with the price of gold in a desperate search for quick (some said 'quack') remedies (Moley, 1939). As the United States was already off the gold standard, this quest for a 'commodity dollar' was inconsequential, and FDR soon abandoned it in favour of a gold reserve act (1934), which fixed the price of gold, devalued the dollar by 40 per cent and boosted recovery by inflation (Leuchtenburg, 1963; Schlesinger, 1959). By the end of the First Hundred Days, it was clear that the budget could not be balanced; as Perkins (1947, p. 219) explained, FDR 'wanted a balanced budget, but he also wanted to do the right thing by his unemployed fellow citizens.' Nevertheless, Roosevelt always had a guilty conscience about the unbalanced budget (Tugwell, 1969).

In the Congressional elections of November 1934, the Democrats achieved the unusual feat of increasing their majority in mid-term. For Roosevelt, consistently more popular than either the New Deal or his party, it was a personal triumph. His picture was everywhere, his mail for one week exceeded Hoover's for a year, and he was seen and heard constantly all over the country. Roosevelt had been 'all but crowned by the people' (W. A. White, in Schlesinger, 1959, p. 507).

Not everyone was satisfied. The Republicans were demoralized, depleted and divided after so many defeats, but their traditional supporters, the businessmen, began to agitate for a return to laissez-faire and a balanced budget as early as the autumn of 1933. They demanded an end to the New Deal's courtship with labour and its cosseting of the unemployed, and a restoration of business influence at Washington. The New Deal's irksome regulations, competitive projects and corkscrew policies irritated them and inhibited 'confidence' and investment. Perkins (1947, pp. 126, 265) observed that Roosevelt 'never understood the point of view of the business community, nor could he make out why it didn't like him.' FDR believed that business 'should be conducted partly for the welfare of the country as well as to make money' and could never comprehend what drove businessmen to accumulate gargantuan fortunes. He felt that business offered little constructive advice and that he was 'the best friend the profit system ever had' (Davis, 1986, p. 372).

The very rich organized a Liberty League (April 1934) in defence of private property, unlimited profits and unbridled individualism. It denounced FDR as 'a traitor to his class', warned of uncontrolled inflation, crippling taxation and the sapping of the moral fibre of the poor by New Deal handouts. While tasteless sniggers about 'the cripple in the White House' circulated among 'gentlemen in well-warmed and well-stocked clubs' (Roosevelt Papers, 1935, p. 474), the Liberty League solemnly championed the Constitution, though in practice it represented only a handful of East Coast multi-millionaires and their henchmen like Al Smith.

A particularly sore point with businessmen was Section 7a of the National Industrial Recovery Act, permitting collective bargaining, though in practice it proved a toothless beast. Nevertheless, the miners' and other unions campaigned vigorously under the misleading slogan 'The President wants you to join the Union.' They met traditional employer hostility (aided by the forces of law and order) and a rash of bitter and violent strikes broke out in 1934. Roosevelt, who had dealt amicably with navy yard unions twenty years earlier, was 'well-disposed' (Perkins, 1947, p. 248) towards labour, but essentially as a 'patron'. He feared a flourishing, independent Big Labour movement since it might clash with Big Business in a climactic class struggle to the detriment of the public interest. 'There were many things about trade unions that Roosevelt never fully understood,' recalled Perkins (1947, p. 263). 'I doubt that he understood what solidarity means to the trade union movement.' Thus he refused to support the strikers or strengthen 7a. By the beginning of 1935, labour was almost as fed up with the New Deal as was business (Schlesinger, 1959).

Symbolic of the frenetic quest for instant remedies and of the New Deal's tardiness in reaching the destitute was the End Poverty In California movement headed by the muck-raking socialist novelist Upton Sinclair, which very nearly brought him the California governorship. EPIC proposed a state-sponsored 'work-in' by the unemployed to produce and exchange essentials among themselves (McElvaine, 1984). In the South, desperate sharecroppers, black and white, came together in the Southern Tenant Farmers' Union (July 1934) to protest at landlord monopolization of AAA benefits; they met only violent local suppression and no sympathy from Washington.

Much more significant were the demagogues Huey Long and Father Coughlin, and their antithesis, the mild, moralistic Dr Francis Townsend. Long, a pudgy, flamboyant political prodigy from Louisiana, had created there something akin to a South American populist dictatorship before leaving the Governorship for the Senate. More genuinely reformist and less bigoted than others of his genre, Long had been an early, vociferous and occasionally embarrassing supporter of FDR in 1932 and fully expected to be in the President's inner circle. Roosevelt, bracketing him with General MacArthur as one of the two most dangerous men in America (Tugwell, 1969), intuitively sensed a self-appointed Crown Prince and kept Long at a distance. Long, aggrieved and contrasting the New Deal's tenderness towards the money changers with its indifference to the destitute, founded 'Share Our Wealth' to make a radical redistribution of the nation's wealth. Promoted with headline-stealing antics and a sure political touch, its membership may have totalled eight million by 1934. Promising a lump sum of $5000 and a minimum annual income of $2000, Long appealed to the 50 per cent of Americans earning less than that. Though his remedies were 'a mixture of the conventional, the contradictory, the glib and the impractical' (Badger, in Baskerville and Willett, 1986, p. 91), Long, in his early forties and a consummate politician unrivalled save by FDR, posed a potentially decisive threat to Roosevelt's re-election in 1936 and appeared a plausible heir apparent for 1940.

Father Charles E. Coughlin, parish priest turned magnetic broadcaster, was a mid-western populist who had also lauded Roosevelt but found himself excluded from real influence. 'Rich, melodic and authoritative' over the air (Leuchtenburg, 1963, p. 100), he commanded a weekly audience exceeding ten million for his simple inflationary remedies. The New Deal, dubbed initially 'Christ's Deal', quickly became 'the Jew Deal', and Coughlin's splenetic rhetoric appealed widely to those still unreached by the New Deal. Increasingly anti-semitic, forming a National Union for

Social Justice (November 1934), Coughlin drifted alarmingly towards an alliance with Long. Of more immediate concern to Roosevelt was the mushroom success of Townsend's 'Old Age Revolving Pensions'. Senior citizens rarely enjoyed pensions and many were destitute. Townsend, an ageing, impecunious doctor, mobilized them by the million, proposing a $200 monthly pension, to be spent before the next instalment. Raised from sales taxes, it would rescue the elderly from indigence and boost purchasing power. Clubs sprang up nationwide, Congressmen were harassed into supporting the plan, and Townsend, preaching old-fashioned values, led an army of 'Bible-belt solid Americans' (Leuchtenburg, 1963, p. 105) in demanding half of the national income for 10 per cent of the population. Denounced by economists as ruinously impractical, the proposal answered the needs of millions, and 'the sudden upsurge of Townsendism was the striking political phenomenon of 1935' (Schlesinger, 1960, p. 40).

The Second Hundred Days, Spring and Summer 1935

The threatening march of the indigent and indignant had a predictable effect on the politically acute Roosevelt. Steadily gathering together a new programme, he regained the political initiative in the spring of 1935 with a series of 'must' bills. The 'Second Hundred Days' had no more intellectual coherence than the First, but the measures were more carefully drafted. Capitalizing on the more liberal Congress elected in November 1934, they marked New Dealism's high tide. 'Boys, this is our hour,' exclaimed Hopkins. 'We've got to get everything we want in the way of relief, social security, minimum wages' (Leuchtenburg, 1963, p. 117). Hopkins headed the new Works Progress Administration with an initial appropriation of $1.39 billion; it spent eventually over $10 billion and employed an average of 3.5 million, about one-third of the unemployed. While it was attacked by progressives as inadequate, conservatives criticized it for waste and political corruption. However, its funds were 'among the best-spent billions of Roosevelt's New Deal' (McElvaine, 1984; Romasco, 1983, p. 65). Local organization was often inefficient, and there was little forward planning, but its programmes were frequently imaginative, often a boon to communities, and it was comprehensive in occupational coverage and conferred long-term benefits. It sponsored Federal Theater,

Writers', Music and Arts Projects and a Living Newspaper (an American 'agitprop', but a generally conservative one) and undertook a wide range of small-scale public works. A National Youth Administration helped to put youngsters through college.

Rural relief was channelled through a Resettlement Administration headed by Tugwell, though he was dismayed to inherit the archaic 'back-to-the-land' subsistence homesteads, and several farm relief agencies. Its principal object was to settle families from worn-out farms on virgin land, teaching them sensible farming practices. Many farmers received emergency and rehabilitation funds, but only 5,000 were resettled. Migrants found model transit camps and blacks enjoyed relative equality, but the star project was the building of model satellite towns on the edges of great cities. Only three 'greenbelt cities' were built, but they were well designed, well serviced and well housed communities. The Resettlement Administration was never popular with Congress because Tugwell was regarded (wrongly) as an eccentric professor, blacks were treated well, and communitarian experiments were falsely equated with communism. The National Resources Committee (the title varied) stimulated city and regional planning and inventoried resources, but Congress frowned on national planning.

Roosevelt intended to give all Americans security 'from the cradle to the grave' (Perkins, 1947, p. 229) and from early in the administration Perkins, Hopkins and others began drafting what became the Social Security Act (1935). It provided unemployment pay, old age pensions and a few minor benefits, but half the population was excluded, the benefits were minimal, no pensions were paid until 1942, and health was virtually ignored. Employee contributions had a deflationary effect on the economy, and an increasingly disgruntled Moley (1939, p. 303) described the Act as 'a mess'. It was, however, a major breakthrough, acknowledging national responsibility for the needy and providing a platform for expansion. It testified to FDR's humanitarianism but even more to his political wisdom. Employees' contributions gave them a stake in it, so that 'no damn politician can ever scrap my social security program' (Leuchtenburg, 1963, p. 133), and it was popular and efficiently administered. Frances Perkins (1947, p. 243) recalled that 'he always regarded the Social Security Act as the cornerstone of his administration and, I think, took greater satisfaction from it than from anything else.'

Roosevelt clipped the wings of the rich a little with redistributive taxes on inheritance, gifts, corporate earnings, undistributed profits and large incomes, but the proposals were timid, and were diluted further in Congress. The package, largely symbolic, 'neither soaked the rich, penalized bigness, or significantly helped balance the budget' (Conkin, 1967, p. 65), but it certainly angered the wealthy. More significantly, banking reforms strengthened the Federal Reserve Board in Washington at the expense of Wall Street; 'the change in the financial system was enormous,' concluded Tugwell (1969, p. 369). The toughest battle was over the Public Utilities Holding Companies Act. From New York days, Roosevelt had been determined to eliminate holding companies which, superimposed upon the producing company, milked it of profits and kept power rates high. Central to the bill was a 'death sentence' clause guillotining holding companies. A $1 billion power trusts propaganda campaign was countered by a Senate investigation of their behaviour. Congress stalled, and the death sentence was partly commuted, but holding companies were effectively curbed (Conkin, 1967).

The one great measure which was not out of the White House stable was the National Labor Relations Act. Sponsored by New York's liberal Senator Robert F. Wagner, a long-standing friend both of labour and of FDR, it was a true 'Magna Carta' for the unions. Pinning the responsibility for industrial disputes firmly on management, it confirmed all the Section 7a rights and at last made them enforceable in the courts. FDR was 'hardly consulted about it ... It did not particularly appeal to him ... All credit for it belongs to Wagner' (Perkins, 1947, p. 193). Roosevelt thought it unduly favoured labour, and contemplated a veto; many union leaders were indifferent. FDR seems to have been ignorant of the potential labour vote (Morgan, 1985) but finally backed it because it was likely to pass and because he needed Wagner's support on other bills. Thus, despite the act's 'palpable one-sidedness' (Moley, 1939, p. 304), Roosevelt became 'quite unwittingly' (Burns, 1956, p. 215) the father of the new labour movement. Labour benefited from the Wagner Act and from the competition between the craft unions of the American Federation of Labor and the industrial unions of the breakaway Congress of Industrial Organizations; membership climbed from less than three million in 1933 to about nine million in 1939. Big Labour now joined Big Business and Big Government in a trinity overshadowing American life.

Historians have inevitably compared the First and Second

Hundred Days. Moley (1939), Schlesinger (1960, p. 385) and Tugwell (1969) identify them with the First and Second New Deals. 'The year 1935,' pronounced Schlesinger magisterially, 'marked a watershed. In this year the strategy and tactics of the New Deal experienced a subtle but pervasive change.' The Brains Trusters, standard-bearers for Theodore Roosevelt's holistic 'New Nationalism' were replaced, he claims, by the advocates of Woodrow Wilson's atomistic 'New Freedom'; government–business co-operation gave way to government–business conflict. Schlesinger's scenario is far too neat. FDR does not seem to have recognized any sharp alteration of course and maintained a strong continuity in personnel and programmes. Moreover, he never sold out to any one ideology. Thus, though irked by the strident and frequently personal business criticism, and intent on clipping the wings of the business fraternity (as in the Securities and Exchange legislation and the Public Utilities Holding Companies Act), he never abandoned hope of a harmonious relationship with business, and sought the continuation of NRA in some form. It is true that the programmes of the Second Hundred Days in part responded to the needs and pleas of the disadvantaged – the poor, the elderly, the unemployed and organized labour – but the tax reforms, social welfare and WPA measures did nothing specifically for sharecroppers, women, blacks and many occupational groups, and stopped far short of radical demands. In short, the Second Hundred Days marks no clear-cut, deliberate, ideologically based shift from one form of New Dealism to another; as Burns (1956) notes, 1935 represents a masterly Presidential balancing act between the pressures of liberalism and conservatism. Davis (1986, pp. 511–12) catches the essence of the Second Hundred Days; it 'meant no drastic, immediately obvious change of direction ... it amounted to little more than a shift of emphasis among programmes and proposals already in hand.' In the spring of 1935, Roosevelt caught a second wind, ceased drifting, responded to both radical and conservative currents and brought to port plans embarked earlier (Leuchtenburg in Garraty, 1970; McElvaine, 1984).

The Triumph of 1936

After the Second Hundred Days, Roosevelt instituted a short 'breathing spell' to conciliate business, terminating it in his Annual

38

Message of 3 January 1936 (Roosevelt Papers, 1936, p. 16), declaring war upon 'our resplendent economic autocracy' and setting the theme for his re-election campaign. However, he was slow to follow this up, and permitted the Republicans to re-form behind Alfred M. Landon, the attractive, successful and moderately progressive Governor of Kansas. In contrast to Landon's vigorous barnstorming, 'the President smiles and sails and fishes and the rest of us worry and fume,' complained the ever anxious Ickes (1953, I, p. 639). The Republican old guard, however, gradually suppressed Landon's mild liberalism and left Roosevelt all of the middle ground. 'The New Deal,' commented Conkin (1967, p. 83), 'was wonderfully blessed by its enemies.' The homegrown radicals collapsed even more completely, Long, their natural candidate, having been assassinated in September 1935. Coughlin became increasingly anti-semitic, and Townsend, though peaking in 1936, was hurt by financial wrangles. The radicals' Union Party flew apart almost at once. The election turned into 'one long victory parade' (Schlesinger, 1960, p. 630) for the President. Rhetorical denunciations of the 'economic royalists' apart (Roosevelt Papers, 1936, p. 232), Roosevelt simply capitalized on the steady climb out of the depression and the New Deal's widespread benefits. 'It was impossible to be explicit about future plans because there were no future plans,' commented the caustic Moley (1939, p. 351). Identifying himself as the embodiment of liberalism, Roosevelt demanded a blank cheque. 'There is one issue in this campaign,' he told Moley. 'It's myself, and people must be either for me or against me' (Moley, 1939, p. 343).

The 'little people' – farmers, workers, the unemployed, blacks and students – were for him. He polled 27.5 million votes to 16.7 million for Landon and won majorities in forty-six states; only Maine and Vermont went for Landon, who 'went down the creek in a torrent' (W. A. White, in Schlesinger, 1960, p. 642). In Congress, Democrats, riding home on Roosevelt's 'coattails', overwhelmed the Republicans by 75–17 in the Senate and 334–89 in the House. The triumph was a tribute to FDR's masterly timing, intuitive rapport with ordinary Americans, constant visibility, and shrewd distribution of offices and benefits to a wide spectrum – judgeships to Jews, major Federal posts to blacks, relief to the unemployed, subsidies to farmers, union rights to labour. Northern black voters (they were disfranchised in the South) shifted dramatically from the Republicans, the party of emancipation, to the Democrats from

1934. They gained less than whites from the New Deal, and civil rights, apart from a few gestures by Eleanor Roosevelt and Ickes, were not in its lexicon, yet by 1938, 85 per cent of black voters were solidly Democratic; Roosevelt had, indirectly, offered them enough to change their allegiance (McElvaine, 1984; Sitkoff, 1978).

Women occupied a curiously ambivalent position in the New Deal. There were no programmes directed specifically towards them and, as with blacks, any gains they made were the general benefits from the NRA, TVA, Social Security and relief programmes. Like blacks, they suffered discrimination in employment and in wages. Roosevelt himself was not an outspoken advocate of female equality but he was more progressive than most men of his time, nor was his liberalism merely a facet of his well-known political opportunism. It is true that he had quickly realized women made up over half of the electorate after 1920 and impressed the fact on his party. However, he offered no policies geared particularly to women's needs; rather than legislative measures on their behalf, he encouraged women to participate in political life themselves, as candidates and officials. He had no inhibitions about appointing able women to high posts – Mary Harriman Rumsey in NRA and Mary McLeod Bethune (who was black and hence one of the 'doubly-disadvantaged') in NYA, for example – and he was determined to be the first President to seat a woman in the Cabinet. In this endeavour he was fortunate to have at hand the capable, experienced, energetic and socially-concerned Frances Perkins. She was a major figure in the labour, relief and welfare programmes of the New Deal and, with Molly Dewson, head of the Women's Division of the Democratic National Committee, a highly effective election campaigner (Perkins, 1947; Ware, 1981 and 1982).

Equally enthusiastic in politicking was Eleanor Roosevelt, thrust onto the national political stage by Louis Howe to keep FDR's career alive after his polio attack. She graduated into a formidable political figure in her own right, a tireless party worker but also a keen and sometimes wearisome dabbler in social welfare and reform. Ickes, not surprisingly, was particularly infuriated by her meddling. 'I wish Mrs. Roosevelt would stick to her knitting,' he wrote in exasperation (1954, II, p. 64). Previous First Ladies had done just that, but Eleanor was a maverick in the White House – when she was there. Much of the time she was criss-crossing the country, opening New Deal projects, descending coal mines, crawling into migrants' hovels, and always presenting Franklin with detailed and invaluable accounts of the state of the nation. He listened patiently to her pleas on behalf of the downtrodden and heard views he would not have encountered otherwise from labour leaders and social workers whom she had patronized – but he did not take her into his political confidence more than anyone else, which is to say, very little. Eleanor was immensely energetic, patient and gracious, deeply humanitarian and often naïve, but thoroughly determined; she was, in short, the conscience of the New Deal. After FDR's death, she enjoyed an Indian summer as an international stateswoman in her own right. By any standard, she was one of the great women of this century (Hareven, 1968; Eleanor Roosevelt, 1949; Tugwell, 1969).

Second Term Blues, 1937–1939

Roosevelt chose not to make the Supreme Court an election issue. The ultimate constitutional arbiter of all legislation, the Court traditionally displayed a restrained conservatism. Restraint was abandoned on the coming of the New Deal; of ten cases decided in 1935–6, the New Deal won one, drew one and lost eight. The legislation was unprecedented in peacetime and hastily drafted; it fared badly in the lower courts, and the Supreme Court's 1932–4 judgements offered conflicting precedents. In the Schecter case (1935) the Court held by nine votes to nil that the National Industrial Recovery Act interfered with commerce within the states and involved excessive delegations of power to the President and trade associations. The Butler decision (1936) invalidating the Agricultural Adjustment Act by six votes to three declared that agriculture was reserved to the states and that the processing tax was a misuse of the taxing power, since it was regulatory rather than raising revenue. TVA survived, but only by a 5–4 margin. Maidment (in Baskerville and Willett, 1986) has argued that the judges responded judicially rather than politically; they were as bewildered as anyone by the depression and the complexity of modern life – hence their inconsistencies. Roosevelt (and most historians), however, regarded the court as a political body, a substantial part of which was determined to destroy the New Deal and frustrate the general will. Most writers identify three factions on the Court – four die-hard conservatives, three liberals of varying stripe and two 'swingmen', including Chief Justice Charles Evans Hughes, whose votes could go to either wing.

41

Roosevelt's apparently jaundiced comments on the Schecter decision were ill received – the Supreme Court was a sacred cow – and he did not risk the issue in the election. Once re-inaugurated, he moved immediately to reform the Court, arguing that the aged justices were inefficient and proposing to add one justice (to a maximum of six) for every one over the age of seventy who did not retire. The President 'believed sincerely that the people were with him' (Ickes, 1954, II, p. 143) but the 'Court-packing bill' met instant and concerted opposition. Congressional leaders resented the peremptory demand to pass a bill on which they had not been consulted and which raised the constitutional issue of judicial independence. Conservatives like Hatton Sumners of Texas took the opportunity to 'cash in their chips' (Burns, 1956, p. 294) and break with the New Deal and Vice-President Garner was in 'open revolt' (Ickes, 1954, II, p. 140). Even progressives deserted the President, some arguing for a constitutional amendment (a lengthy and uncertain process), others fearing for civil liberties. The Republicans cheerfully 'let the Democrats tear each other to pieces' (Ickes, 1954, II, p. 93) and the President's remaining allies lacked confidence.

Hughes dismissed the inefficiency charge in a carefully timed letter and engineered a conservative retirement, giving Roosevelt the opportunity for a liberal nomination but undermining the President's case. In the spring of 1937 the Court upheld the Social Security and National Labor Relations Acts. There seemed little point in pressing on, but FDR's 'Dutch was up' and he fought stubbornly until he was 'driven in ignominious defeat from an untenable position' (Ickes, 1954, II, p. 178). Arrogance, deviousness, incompetence and obstinacy marked his course to defeat; the triumph of 1936 seemed to have gone to his head, and he became a 'political royalist'. He need not have lost. It was generally conceded that the Court itself had behaved arrogantly, but while some urged patience till nature removed the obstructive judges, others called for reforms short of 'packing'. Not all of the debate was high-minded; it was 'a struggle in power politics as well as in the grand principles of government' (Conkin, 1967, p. 92). 'Chief Justice Hughes has played a bad hand perfectly while we have played a good hand badly,' admitted Ickes (1954, II, p. 145). Congressmen took advantage of a President supposedly in his final term and therefore unable to help them in future elections. Roosevelt should have waited to see if the Court followed the election returns and upheld the New

Deal. The defeat 'wasted a Congressional session, helped destroy the Roosevelt myth of invincibility, disillusioned many of his former disciples, divided the Democratic party, gave the Republican party a new lease on life, and left Roosevelt bitter and hurt' (Conkin, 1967, p. 94). He was determined to get even.

Further humiliations followed. A Reorganization Bill (1938) permitting modest and necessary additions to the White House staff was rejected as rampant dictatorship; a milder version passed in 1939 when passions had cooled (Burns, 1956; Conkin, 1967). The Fair Labor Standards Act (1938), setting minimum wages and maximum hours, was mangled by Southern conservatives and lobbyists; only half a million workers benefited (Bernstein, 1970; Perkins, 1947). The Pure Food and Drug Act (1938) was emasculated beyond the point of effectiveness by industry lobbies. A permanent AAA, fat with farm benefits, failed in 1937 but struggled through in 1938. The Farm Security Administration (1937), absorbing the Resettlement Administration, helped tenants to purchase farms but enjoyed limited appropriations thanks to the Southerners. The Housing Act (1937) was a token response to FDR's claim in his second inaugural address that one-third of Americans were ill-housed; a pitiful $500 million was appropriated for public housing. The British economist J. M. Keynes's suggestion of a vast programme to prime the economic pump was disregarded (Conkin, 1967; McElvaine, 1984). The sit-down strikes of 1936–7, in which workers encamped in factories, were effective in forcing collective bargaining but met general disapproval. Businessmen were exasperated by FDR's 'hands-off' attitude to the strikes and by his ambivalence towards business. Ickes (1954, II, p. 326) complained that FDR, after encouraging him to make 'antimonopoly speeches, is pulling petals off the daisy with representatives of big business'. In 1937, Roosevelt reinstituted anti-trust proceedings, and in 1938 the Temporary National Economic Committee investigated business; neither move was effective. FDR may have used them to avoid real action (Conkin, 1967; Moley, 1939) and he always hankered after a permanent NRA. 'The New Deal,' wrote Hofstadter (1955, p. 312), 'never developed a clear or consistent line on business consolidation.'

Worst of all in these nightmare years was the 'Roosevelt Recession' (autumn 1937–spring 1938). Federal expenditures were cut in June 1937 to meet FDR's long-held desire to balance the budget; it was hoped that business would take up the slack. Mindful of Roosevelt's inconsistency, business failed to respond; from August, all the economic indicators plunged in 'the most precipitous economic decline in American history' (Conkin, 1967, p. 96; Romasco, 1983). Unemployment rose from 7.5 to 11 million, social security contributions swallowed $2 billion of the nation's purchasing power, interest rates climbed, and investment, prices and profits fell (Garraty, 1986). Roosevelt drifted. 'He doesn't seem to know just what he can or should do about it,' reported Ickes (1954, II, p. 317) in February 1938. Successive defeats and the bewildering slump appeared to stun him (Morgan, 1985), and he found it impossible to choose between the advice of Treasury Secretary Morgenthau to hold fast to budget balancing and that of the Federal Reserve Board's chief, Marriner Eccles, to return to a measure of Federal deficit spending. However, in April 1938, international dangers, approaching elections and smooth talk from Hopkins pushed FDR into a $2 billion increase in defence spending and $3.75 billion for relief, but recovery was slow; nine million were still jobless when Europe went to war in September 1939 (Garraty, 1986; McElvaine, 1984). The Keynesian lesson, just beginning to be digested in America, was articulated by Perkins (1947, p. 224): 'The principal factor in our economic recovery was the expenditure of public funds for public works, work relief, and agricultural adjustment and resettlement programmes' (see also Baskerville in Baskerville and Willett, 1986; Davis, 1986).

Hopkins was part of the new 'inner circle' developing round the President. Jim Farley (1948, p. 68) was squeezed out: 'White House confidence on politics and policy went to a small band of zealots, who mocked at party loyalty and knew no devotion except unswerving obedience to their leader.' Farley was an old-time party professional; the new men were New Deal ideologues. Hopkins, a brilliant executive, closer to FDR than anyone since Howe's death in 1936, faithfully responsive to his master's voice, was an 'intense, brittle, tactless, irreverent operative' (Burns, 1971, p. 60). 'There was a temperamental sympathy between the two men which made their relationship extremely easy as well as faithful and productive,' remarked Perkins (1947, p. 155). The New Deal was increasingly frustrated from 1937 by a developing though somewhat unstable alliance between conservative Democrats (mostly rural and often Southerners) and Republicans. The new 'inner circle' instituted a 'purge' of Democratic conservatives in the 1938 party primary elections. Roosevelt, despite his long-term aim of gathering all liberals under the Democratic banner and forcing conservatives to join the Republicans, gave little support until a few liberal victories encouraged him to throw Presidential power and prestige behind the Purge. A Fireside Chat (July 1938) on the necessity for a thoroughly liberal Democratic party was followed by a tour round selected states; supposedly vulnerable conservatives were challenged on their home ground; invulnerable ones were ignored. 'Presidential pride was sorely scorched' by the Court bill defeat and Roosevelt was particularly 'furious' over 'Southern betrayal' on the Fair Labor Standards Act and other measures (Farley, 1948, pp. 95, 116). FDR identified the South as 'the Nation's No. 1 economic problem' (Roosevelt Papers, 1938, p. 421), its backward condition seemingly condoned by many of its Congressmen. Conservatives resisted the Purge, Garner labelling it as 'unnecessary as hell' (Farley, 1948, p. 128); almost all of them won their primary heats. Roosevelt's issues were not necessarily local ones, Presidential interference in local elections was resented, and he was vulnerable to charges of dictatorship. Localism was probably too strong to permit reform, but in any case 'he never made the strategic commitment that would allow a carefully considered, thorough and long-term attempt at party reorganization' (Burns, 1956, p. 376). Moreover, he should have built up a more substantial personal organization and avoided going into the states in person.

Conservative Revival and Liberal Coda, 1938–1945

In the elections proper (November 1938), the Republicans gained eight Senate seats and eighty-one in the House. The conservative coalition became general and permanent (Patterson, 1967); it was not broken until Lyndon Johnson's election in 1964. The electorate wished to retain the New Deal's reforms but not to extend them. The conservatives now chipped away at agencies and appropriations; by 1943 all emergency programmes had been scrapped. FDR traded them for support for his increasingly interventionist foreign policy and the concomitant rearmament.

Roosevelt genuinely desired to retire to Hyde Park in January 1941, but the worsening international situation seemed to demand an experienced hand at the tiller, and the conservative revival raised the spectre of a reactionary successor. FDR had discouraged crown princes until 1938, when Hopkins was built up, only to subside through illness. The President told Farley (1948, p. 188) that he wanted 'someone who is sympathetic to my administration and who will continue my policies', but those who were sympathetic lacked political credibility; those who possessed it were unsympathetic. Roosevelt could not, therefore, rule out a third term but he hedged until the eve of the 1940 convention; he was 'genuinely unsure of his own desires' (Burns, 1956, p. 409). Labour and other elements of the New Deal coalition demanded him, and Hitler, sweeping up Europe, prompted him to run. He won nomination virtually unchallenged but had difficulty foisting the liberal Henry Wallace on the party as his running mate. FDR, embroiled in foreign affairs, essayed a relaxed, non-partisan campaign but the Republicans came up with the energetic, appealing, moderately liberal Wendell Willkie and forced the old campaigner onto the stump. In his urban heartlands and at defence plants, Roosevelt displayed the old panache; rising employment and incomes helped him back with another massive majority. Though Willkie proved 'more disturbing to Roosevelt as a rival than anyone who ran against him' (Perkins, 1947, p. 94), he differed too little from FDR to offer a genuine alternative, and Willkie's campaign which began with rumpled zest ended in crumpled exasperation.

Congress remained a stumbling block, the Democratic majority slumping to fourteen in 1942. In 1944 an 'Economic Bill of Rights' was defeated by business lobbies, though a 'GI Bill of Rights' providing disability, health, education, and home loan benefits for twelve million uniformed constituents went through. Having broken tradition in 1940, FDR had little difficulty in securing a fourth term in 1944, though the party dumped Wallace in favour of a professional politician, Senator Harry S. Truman of Missouri. After a brief flirtation with a second party liberalization plan, Roosevelt campaigned as effectively as ever against his most resourceful opponent, Governor Thomas E. Dewey of New York. A stern, unbending 'law-and-order' zealot, Dewey played the 'Red scare' card, and Roosevelt, disgusted at Republican smears, dubbed it 'the dirtiest campaign in all history' (Tugwell, 1969, p. 658). Cushioned by a still comfortable majority, the champion began the last climactic months of his astounding reign. The New Deal reforms were secure, but the war was far from over and the peace a vague sketch.

The New Deal Balance Sheet

If the acid test of anti-depression policies is the extent to which they reduce unemployment, then the New Deal rates five marks out of ten; almost eighteen million were jobless in 1933, and nine million were still unemployed in 1939. Moreover, at any given time, the New Deal assisted only a third of the workless, while, as thousands of blacks, senior citizens and sharecroppers could testify, the 'forgotten man' often remained forgotten (McElvaine, 1983). Other economic indicators recorded better gains, but the economy as a whole remained sluggish until rescued by the war.

Why, at best, only two cheers for the New Deal? Part of the blame rests with Roosevelt. He lacked the will and ability to give the New Deal intellectual coherence and depth. Despite his increasingly radical rhetoric, he made little attempt to tackle the roots of injustice and inequality. He refused whole-hearted commitment to any policy. His measures often served political rather than purely economic and social ends. Lacking an ideological identity and programmatic cohesion, the New Deal became a congeries of often contradictory policies, changing direction sharply and with bewildering frequency and, as D. K. Adams has observed (1982), it was easier to say what it opposed than what it represented.

Nevertheless, the administration was not solely to blame for the New Deal's shortcomings. The Great Depression was totally unprecedented, and there was an 'absence of consensus among economic analysts' (Romasco, 1983, p. 3) as to its causes and remedies; thus 'an era of fumbling and muddling through was inevitable' (Hofstadter, 1967, p. 313). Moreover, the destruction wrought in the previous four years was so complete that even if Roosevelt had struck the right path at once and pursued it steadfastly, almost certainly it would have taken at least eight years to effect a complete repair. Furthermore, for all of the New Deal's bumbling and fudging, 'plausible alternatives ... are not easily suggested, particularly if one considers all the confining and limiting circumstances' (Conkin, 1967, p. 106). Roosevelt had to contend with the fickleness of the American public; support for the New Deal peaked in 1936 and faded rapidly thereafter; most people had gained from it what they wanted. Business in particular offered persistent and redoubtable opposition, while Congress increasingly manifested a mind of its own and Roosevelt's own party, swollen by the President's popularity, balked him consistently in his second term. Implementation of the New Deal at local level was frequently flawed by the inadequacies of its agents (Trout, 1977).

Nevertheless, the New Deal's achievements were profound and

enduring. Relief programmes not only overcame much of the destitution and despair, they bestowed substantial cultural benefits and renewed and expanded much of the nation's infra-structure. Despite the hiccup of the 'Roosevelt Recession', farmers were over 50 per cent better off by 1939, while business and banking were on much sounder footings. Roosevelt recognized this, but business failed to do so. 'The enemies of the New Deal were wrong. They should have been its friends' (Conkin, 1967, p. 74). Government boosts to consumer spending and capital investment together with curbs on malpractices 'conserved and protected American corporate capitalism' (Bernstein, 1970, p. 264). Moreover, big business was balanced to some extent by big labour, and both had to reckon with the countervailing power of big government. America found its way, painfully and tortuously, to a managed economy.

The New Deal united the country physically and spiritually, reaching into all corners of national and individual life. Accepting Federal responsibility for the welfare of all Americans, it taught them to look to Washington and especially the White House in time of crisis, and began to fashion a safety net for the victims of life's vicissitudes. Roosevelt had an unrivalled capacity to think in national (and global) terms, as was demonstrated by his successful rehabilitation of the national estate through his vast conservation schemes and his constant reference to the theme of 'interdependence'.

The greatest limitation on swift, fundamental, consistent and effective action was the nature of America itself. Roosevelt intuitively grasped the pluralist character of American life and the need for a broad consensus among contending interests to defeat the depression, revivify and stabilize the existing social and economic order, iron out inefficiencies and correct at least some of the more glaring injustices. A total politician, he acted as a broker between the interests, granting to each just enough to secure its allegiance without alienating the others. As Pells remarks, 'the key word in the vocabulary of the Roosevelt Administration was "balance"' (1973, p. 79). The measure of his success is his own extraordinary sequence of electoral triumphs and the forging of a 'Roosevelt coalition' which made the Democrats the natural majority party for the next generation. Moreover, as he intended, the New Deal has continued to set the agenda of American politics.

The New Deal gave practical help to most Americans at some time during the 1930s, but Roosevelt's greatest gifts to his people

48

were spiritual ones. While dispensing charity, he gave them renewed faith in their society and the hope of a brighter future. He began by rousing them from the torpor into which the depression had cast them and within a week he had established with them a bond unmatched by any other President. 'I never forget that I live in a house owned by all the American people,' he told them in 1938, 'and that I have been given their trust... And constantly I seek to look ... into the hopes and fears of men and women in their homes.' He concluded confidently, 'I feel sure that your hopes and your help are with me' (Roosevelt Papers, 1938, pp. 247–8). Many came to feel that Lincoln's great ideal of government of the people, by the people and for the people had been realized in practice.

The New Deal was occasioned by the need to overcome the Great Depression, but amid all of the kaleidoscopic turmoil, the tumbling, twisting patterns of policies, politicians, planners, patricians and plebeians, Roosevelt proclaimed a nobler and more enduring aim: 'We are going to make a country in which no one is left out' (Perkins, 1947, p. 92). Under no illusion that he could bring it about in his own time, he nevertheless affirmed the promise made in 1776: life, liberty and the pursuit of happiness. The greatest test of his inspired leadership was yet to come: the achievement of victory in a war against the forces of darkness and the establishment of a just and lasting peace.

4 Roosevelt and World Affairs (1933–1945)

The Search for Peace, 1933–1937

American foreign policy from Independence to Pearl Harbor is generally described as 'isolationist' – inaccurately, for the United States traded extensively, assumed through the Monroe Doctrine (1823) a protective role for the western hemisphere, sought territories and concessions in the Pacific and Far East, and made numerous treaties, though abhorring 'entangling alliances' and retaining political and military freedom of action. 'Open Door' economic penetration blended with a desire to act as a moral exemplar. Following Wilson's failure to secure American membership of the League of Nations, Republican policy (1921–33) adhered to traditional precepts but adapted them to take account of America's new and formidable status, resulting in an 'interwar compromise' (Leopold, 1962, p. 403) between 'isolationism' and 'internationalism'. While retaining freedom of action the Republicans promoted trade, sponsored naval limitation agreements, a Pacific non-aggression pact and the internationalization of the 'Open Door' in China. In the Kellogg–Briand Pact (1928), they induced the rest of the world to renounce war as an instrument of national policy, and they participated in the Geneva World Disarmament Conference (1932). America negotiated a substantial reduction in German reparations, and in Latin America a self-conscious 'Good Neighbor' policy replaced armed intervention. Before 1931, these gentlemanly policies worked well, but then Japan seized Chinese Manchuria. President Hoover merely refused to recognize the acquisition of territory by force, for the American people, preoccupied with the depression, cared little for faraway places.

Franklin Roosevelt, a scion of the cosmopolitan, sophisticated and extrovert 'Eastern Establishment', was well travelled and had extensive foreign connections. A disciple of Theodore Roosevelt's forceful assertion that America must play an active global role, his years in the Wilson administration 'enhanced his alertness to the role of power in foreign affairs' (Cole, 1983, p. 4), fostered his own activism and aroused his support for the League of Nations. His spirited but unavailing championship of American membership during the 1920 Presidential election continued throughout the decade, and he was a prominent spokesman for the study of international relations, membership of the World Court, the reduction of war debts and tariffs, the Good Neighbor policy and disarmament. However, when the depression struck he focused on domestic recovery. Moreover, in order to win over hardline nationalists to his candidacy in 1932, he renounced his pro-League views, at least in public, and foreign policy was not an election issue. Nevertheless, he understood the interdependence of nations and regions, and the links between peace and prosperity, depression and war. He saw that modern technology, especially in the air, was fast abolishing distance and thereby undermining America's historic security. Fearing a two-ocean war in which the United States stood alone, he appreciated that she occupied a central place in contemporary geopolitics. He was determined to run his own foreign policy and be as constructive as circumstances allowed.

FDR had little scope for dramatic policymaking in his first term. He endorsed the non-recognition doctrine, continued the drive for disarmament and made the Good Neighbor policy his own. Preoccupied with domestic recovery from the depression, he assisted world recovery essentially through bilateral trade agreements. Aware of a 'general indifference to outside events' (Divine, 1962, p. 78), he was conscious that New Deal supporters were generally 'isolationists' abroad. Roosevelt's policy was therefore somewhat out of character. He adopted 'a practical day-to-day approach' and 'improvised from one situation to another' (Burns, 1956, pp. 247, 249), seemingly vague of purpose and devoid of interest; but the claim (Divine, 1969, p. 7) that 'Roosevelt pursued an isolationist policy out of genuine conviction' is hardly sustained by the evidence. Roosevelt meant to shape the world his way and bided his time. He was well informed about the aggressors, had no illusions about their ambitions, and built up American naval strength while being prepared to reduce it if other nations co-operated. He revealed his concern at the deteriorating global situation in January 1935: 'I cannot with candor tell you that general international relationships ... are improved ... many old jealousies are resurrected, old passions aroused, new stirrings for armament and power ... rear their ugly heads' (Roosevelt Papers, 1935, p. 24).

His one positive act was recognition of the Soviet Union, a matter of common sense tinged with vain hopes of markets and a Russian curb on Japanese expansion. FDR's bid to join the World Court (January 1935) seemed to have the necessary two-thirds Senate majority, but shrill extremists denounced it as 'a back door entrance to the League' (Divine, 1962, p. 83) and screamed, 'To hell with Europe and the rest of those nations!' (Dallek, 1979, p. 95). As was to become a familiar pattern, FDR retreated once substantial opposition arose. A further and sharper setback followed. FDR wished to avoid being dragged into war the way Wilson had been in 1917. He therefore approved a ban on loans to belligerents in 1934 and encouraged a Senate investigation of the arms trade. However, matters got out of hand. A peace movement several million strong demonstrated and lobbied. A magazine labelled Great War profiteers 'The Merchants of Death', and 'revisionist' historians charged that business and Allied propaganda had misled America into an unnecessary war. Darkening skies abroad combined with this agitation to produce the 1935 Neutrality Act. Roosevelt supported an arms embargo and a ban on travel on belligerent ships and in war zones, but wished to retain discretion in favour of victims of aggression. He failed, for once, to persuade a Congress nervous of the vociferous peace lobby, and was forced to accept a 'scissors and paste' act (Cole, 1983, pp. 178–9) which gave him no discretion whatsoever and which abandoned the neutral rights to which America clung so tenaciously between 1914 and 1917. A 1936 amendment banned loans to belligerents completely, and in 1937 a bizarre two-year 'cash and carry' clause permitted belligerents to purchase American goods (except arms) for cash, transporting them in their own vessels. The nation realized that total economic self-denial in a war threatened prosperity, yet thought it could stay at peace by staying at home. FDR had scarcely more room for manoeuvre than in 1935.

The Italian invasion of Ethiopia in 1935 tested revisionist neutrality. Roosevelt, seeking to bolster League opposition to the Italian aggression, called for a moral embargo on all trade with Italy, particularly oil supplies. 'An effective embargo on petrol products would have crippled the Italian war effort within a few weeks'

(Divine, 1962, p. 127), but, to Roosevelt's chagrin, oil and other goods flowed to Italy in increased quantities (even more so from Europe); the 'merchants of death' ignored the President's plea to forego their profits. At the same time, the final attempt at disarmament failed. The London Naval Conference (1935) collapsed when Japan, refused parity with Britain and the United States, walked out and promptly announced a naval expansion; Britain and America followed suit, and world talk henceforth was of rearmament.

By the end of his first term, 'Roosevelt had found no effective means to serve the cause of peace' (Dallek, 1979, p. 121), and the only cause for congratulation was the growing amity with Latin America. America's new benignity was not yet completely trusted, but the southern republics welcomed it, and it paid good economic dividends. In August 1936, Roosevelt contrasted hemispheric good neighbourliness with the threats to peace elsewhere and offered 'to every Nation of the world the handclasp of the good neighbor'. Speaking to the pacificistic Chautauqua movement, he declared, 'I have seen war... I hate war,' drawing sustained applause (Roosevelt Papers, 1936, pp. 289, 292). It may have been 'a clear and precise statement of his innermost beliefs' (Divine, 1969, p. 10) but it is better seen as 'part of his continuing efforts to win and retain the political support of Western progressives' (Cole, 1983, p. 200). Moreover, he warned ominously that no neutrality, however complete, could guarantee peace.

The Road to War, 1937–1941

Even before Roosevelt returned to the White House, the Spanish Civil War (1936–9) threatened to engulf Europe. Roosevelt knew he ought to help the Spanish government, but the combined effects of Anglo-French supineness, Catholic and isolationist opinion in an election year, public indifference, and America's fervent wish to stay at peace prevented him from doing so, and the arms embargo was extended to civil wars in 1937. 'He was ready to accept a Franco victory rather than risk a wider war' (Dallek, 1979, p. 143).

Roosevelt confessed in 1936 that 'the whole European panorama is fundamentally blacker than at any time in your life ... or mine,' and a year later it was said that 'the President's attitude is one of complete helplessness about the European situation' (Dallek, 1979, pp. 122, 138). Though FDR now believed that Hitler aimed at world conquest (an opinion strengthened by Germany's economic challenge in the western hemisphere), given America's traditional resolve to avoid Europe's parochial quarrels, he could only encourage Britain and France to restrain Hitler. He attempted to cultivate Britain's new Prime Minister, Neville Chamberlain, but they had little respect for each other. Nevertheless, he congratulated Chamberlain on preserving peace at Munich (30 September 1938), though he feared that appeasement merely delayed hostilities. The Nazi digestion of the rump of Czechoslovakia in March 1939 angered him greatly (Dallek, 1979); war now seemed inevitable, and, feeling it was unlikely that America could long remain at peace, Roosevelt took tentative steps to align America with Britain and France. As early as January 1938, he sanctioned covert Anglo-American naval talks, and after Munich permitted France to buy American warplanes. He also told Chamberlain that he could count on 'the industrial resources of the American nation behind him in the event of war' (Reynolds, 1981, p. 47). By January 1939 he was hinting that America's frontier lay on the Rhine (inducing charges of warmongering and toadying to the British), and he warned the Axis powers obliquely, 'We, too, have a stake in world affairs' (Dallek, 1979, p. 185).

In Europe Roosevelt confronted aggression only indirectly, but in Asia he was brought face to face with it. In July 1937, Japan invaded China, and Roosevelt had to decide whether to appease the Japanese by sacrificing China, whether to continue the almost equally lame non-recognition doctrine, or whether to get tough with the aggressor – or to find some way of expressing disapproval of Japan which would stiffen Chinese resistance, strengthen moderate elements in Japan, issue a veiled warning to the warlords there and unite American opinion behind him. He determined to test public opinion in isolationism's citadel, Chicago, in October 1937. 'Let no one imagine that America will escape' a general war, he warned, for 'There is a solidarity and interdependence about the modern world, both technical and moral, which makes it impossible for any nation completely to isolate itself from economic and political upheavals in the rest of the world.' However, he carefully avoided naming the aggressors and called vaguely for a 'quarantine' against them 'to protect the health of the community against the spread of the disease' (Roosevelt Papers, 1937, pp. 409–10). This ambiguous address has led to much speculation. Divine (1962, p. 211) argues that it 'marked a radical shift in Roosevelt's outlook on world affairs', which is patently not the case; he is on firmer ground in stating (1969, pp. 18–19) that it 'marks the beginning of Roosevelt's long campaign to wean his fellow-countrymen away from the extreme isolationism of the mid-1930's'. The speech was a trial balloon rather than a statement of policy. It represents also 'a change in the relative weight and priority given to domestic and foreign policy' (Cole, 1983, p. 243). Initial reaction favoured a firmer line abroad, but the formidable isolationist lobby rallied and Roosevelt judged the time unripe for overt acts to deter aggressors. Wilson's spectre stood always at his side. 'It is a terrible thing,' he said, 'to look over your shoulder when you're trying to lead – and to find no one there' (Burns, 1956, pp. 318–19).

Nevertheless, 'the war in China caused many Americans to realise that they did have a genuine interest in the course of events overseas' (Divine, 1962, p. 219). Roosevelt was able to ignore the Neutrality Act as war had not been declared, but while he pushed for 'everything . . . we can get away with' in the form of aid to China (Dallek, 1979, p. 237), little went to Chiang Kai-shek, and Japan benefited more from the unrestricted trade than China. Moreover, moral support for China was balanced by a fervent desire to avoid provoking Japan. When Japan wilfully mistreated Westerners in China, Washington's voice was muffled, and even when a US gunboat was sunk in an unprovoked attack, the public was relieved when Japan responded to FDR's protest with an apology.

There were, however, signs that the nation's faith in its ability to insulate itself from world events was on the wane. In the winter of 1937–8, Roosevelt was able to persuade Congress to authorize a two-ocean navy. Impressed by the development of intercontinental aircraft, which rendered America vulnerable to bombing, he pressed, though with less success, for a strong home air defence and a strategic bomber force as a deterrent. The isolationists, unmoved by increasing evidence that neutralism was no longer possible, proposed a constitutional amendment requiring a referendum before a declaration of war. The 'Ludlow Amendment', strongly supported by peace groups, polled impressively in Congress, but by strenuous efforts the administration defeated it. 'If the House vote revealed isolationist strength,' observes Cole (1983, p. 253), 'it also revealed President Roosevelt's growing power relative to the isolationists.'

Though Roosevelt had declared that 'America actively engages in the search for peace' (Roosevelt Papers, 1937, p. 411), he was little more than a bystander when Europe blundered into war. Concerned that the existing neutrality legislation was calculated to provoke war rather than promote peace, he allowed Senator Pittman, chairman of the Senate Foreign Relations Committee, to attempt to amend it in May 1939, but, apparently feeling that the move was premature, refused to throw his weight behind it, and the bid failed. His neutrality proclamation on the outbreak of the European war (September 1939) nevertheless carried a moral commitment to the Allies. 'Even a neutral,' he said, 'cannot be asked to close his mind or his conscience,' adding that 'the peace of all countries everywhere is in danger' (Roosevelt Papers, 1939, pp. 461, 463). He now drove hard for neutrality revision, exploiting the leverage of war, though the isolationists still fought hard. The arms embargo was repealed, and the cash and carry provision extended indefinitely; the Allies could now draw upon America's vast resources – as long as their money lasted.

During the ensuing 'phoney war' (September 1939 to April 1940), Roosevelt despatched Under-Secretary of State Welles to Europe on a peace mission. FDR probably realized that it would be fruitless, but it demonstrated his commitment to peace and may have been designed to delay a decisive German attack and persuade Mussolini to stay on the sidelines. More significantly, he invited Chamberlain and Churchill (the new First Lord of the Admiralty) to correspond freely with him. The Chamberlain invitation was probably a courtesy; Churchill was his real target 'because there is a strong possibility that he will become prime minister' (Kimball, 1984, p. 7). Churchill was dynamic and belligerent; moreover, the contact was a logical development from the naval staff talks, especially as Roosevelt believed that continued friendly control of the Atlantic was vital to America's security.

FDR's support for the Allies during this period must not be overestimated. Disappointed by the Allies' limp failure to court Russia, he was revolted by the Nazi–Soviet Pact and disgusted by Russia's seizure of the Baltic republics and most of Poland; more particularly, he was 'not only horrified but thoroughly angry' (Dallek, 1979, p. 209) at her assault on Finland. Even so, he was careful not to aid the Finns effectively lest he should cement the Hitler–Stalin bond.

Only after the shock of the fall of France, the climax of Hitler's devastatingly successful blitzkrieg in the spring of 1940, did FDR begin, haltingly, to offer the tottering Allies something more than strong verbal support. The swing towards a more active role developed slowly during the summer. Thus in June, condemning Mussolini's attack on mortally-wounded France, he exploded, 'The hand that held the dagger has struck it into the back of its neighbor,' but ignored Allied pleas for American armed intervention (Roosevelt Papers, 1940, p. 263). Moreover, he was reluctant to supply Britain with arms additional to those already on order, because of America's own flimsy defences and until he was assured either that Britain would survive or, if defeated, that her fleet would not be surrendered. The Battle of Britain found Roosevelt running for re-election; he was anxious not to give his opponents ammunition by wasting munitions on a shaky Britain. He did take one significant step which indicated a more positive American attitude – the transfer of French arms contracts to the United Kingdom – but when a desperate Churchill pleaded for the sale of fifty over-age American destroyers, Roosevelt stalled, seeking assurances about Britain's capacity to survive and save the fleet. Furthermore, he did not know how the transfer could be accomplished constitutionally, nor did he know how to justify the reduction of America's inadequate anti-submarine forces. The deal went through only after the Battle of Britain swung Britain's way. British western hemisphere bases were leased to the USA in return for the destroyers. Roosevelt was quick to tell his people that he had pulled off a good deal; it was less a contribution to Allied defences than the completion of a defensive membrane round the Americas. However, he took 'a colossal political risk' (Burns, 1971, p. 441) in boldly pushing it through in the midst of a re-election campaign. The old destroyers, though slow to come into service, played a significant role in the Battle of the Atlantic in 1941–2, and Churchill rightly described the deal as 'a decidedly unneutral act by the United States' (Reynolds, 1981, p. 132) and welcomed it as a giant stride towards American semi-belligerency, which he deemed the minimum necessary to defeat Hitler. All in all, it represented a considerable moral victory for British diplomacy and propaganda, and for Churchill.

By the autumn of 1940, therefore, Americans were prepared to give the Allies moral support, especially if it could be shown to be America's best defence, but peace remained even more precious to them. The Committee to Defend America by Aiding the Allies represented this view, but the 850,000-strong America First movement argued that aid denuded 'Fortress America' and was pointless since the Allies were doomed. Leading Senatorial isolationists were prominent members, but its star was the heroic Atlantic flyer Charles Lindbergh, as charismatic as Roosevelt. Lindbergh was 'particularly formidable and worrisome' (Cole, 1983, p. 459), but in the autumn of 1940 the President was harassed more by his Republican opponent Wendell Willkie, nominally an internationalist but tempted to play the isolationist card as polling day loomed. Roosevelt, normally exceedingly cautious, was panicked into a statement which came back to haunt him in 1941: 'I have said this before, but I shall say it again and again and again: Your boys are not going to be sent into any foreign wars' (Roosevelt Papers, 1940, p. 517). Events and Roosevelt's increasingly vehement responses to them quickly undermined this promise. As British and Chinese fortunes waned, Roosevelt stepped further towards belligerency, taking two Republican internationalists into his cabinet (June 1940) and at Christmas announcing, 'We must be the great arsenal of democracy' and saying that it was 'of the most vital concern to us that the European and Asian war-makers should not gain control of the oceans which lead to this hemisphere' (Roosevelt Papers, 1940, pp. 607, 643).

As Roosevelt aligned America irrevocably with Britain, 'the chief business between our two countries,' recalled Churchill, 'was virtually conducted by these interchanges between him and me' (Lash, 1977, p. 183). Of similar backgrounds, idiosyncratic, resolute, lovers of power and of the limelight, candid yet informal, by the beginning of 1941 they had forged 'A Common-Law Alliance' (Sherwood, 1948, p. 264). Harry Hopkins, dubbed 'Lord-Root-of-the-Matter' by Churchill, became 'a catalytic agent between two prima donnas' (Sherwood, 1948, p. 237). Yet this emerging alliance faced a major crisis in December 1940, when Churchill warned Roosevelt that Britain would soon run out of dollars. FDR responded with the Lend-Lease Act, skilfully piloted through a still hesitant Congress in March 1941, by which goods were lent or leased to Britain (and later other allies) in the illusory expectation that they would be returned or compensated for after the war. Lend-Lease became 'the linch-pin of the Anglo-American relationship' during the war (Dobson, 1986, p. 1). For Roosevelt, it represented 'very nearly an act of war' (Divine, 1969, p. 40) but 'we will not be intimidated by the threats of the dictators that they will regard as a breach of international law or as an act of war our aid to the democracies who dare to resist their aggression' (Roosevelt Papers, 1940, p. 669). It also represented 'an extraordinary grant of power to the executive' (Kimball, 1973, p. 49), testimony to the distance FDR had been permitted to travel by the exigencies of war. Nevertheless, he still described Lend-Lease as an integral part of 'our rearming process' (Roosevelt Papers, 1940, p. xxx). Churchill referred to it as 'the most unsordid legislative act' in history (Lash, 1977, p. 289) but it led ultimately to 'a relationship of competitive co-operation' (Reynolds, 1981, p. 294) in which many conflicting ambitions remained as each power jostled for postwar commercial advantage. America exercised her increasingly overwhelming economic strength and exacted a heavy price for Lend-Lease; in due course, the British had to agree to co-ordinate postwar economic policy with the United States, which sought the dismantling of Empire Preference in favour of a universal Open Door policy (Gardner, 1964; Kimball, 1969). 'Lend-Lease,' concludes Dobson (1986, p. 225), 'was an act of generosity unsurpassed in its magnitude; but the United States was determined to get a payment from Britain in terms of commitments to economic policies which were conducive to American interests.'

Having secured his financial lifeline, Churchill next hoped to meet Roosevelt to persuade him into untrammelled belligerency by the summer of 1941. Roosevelt wished to charm Churchill into supporting American ideals. Each was curious about the other. Aboard warships off Newfoundland (August 1941) they met at last and drew up in the Atlantic Charter a statement of common aims for the postwar world. They abjured territorial gains, championed self-determination, affirmed an economic open door, sought improved standards of living, a secure peace, freedom of the seas and disarmament, and endorsed Roosevelt's 'Four Freedoms' – freedom from want and fear and freedom of worship and expression (Roosevelt Papers, 1940, p. 672; 1941, p. 314). Their main business, however, was to refine their common strategy. Based on the American 'Plan Dog' (November 1940), informally agreed to by British staff officers in January 1941, it identified Germany as the most dangerous foe; the corollary of this 'Europe First' strategy was that in the increasingly likely event of a two-ocean war, they would stand on the defensive against Japan until Germany was defeated. Roosevelt still hoped that all aid short of war would be sufficient to assure an Allied victory, but if America was forced to intervene, he (unlike his staff) believed her participation could be limited to aerial and maritime warfare.

As British shipping losses reached critical levels in 1941, Roosevelt inched towards war at sea, charting his course by constant reference to public opinion. The British ambassador, Lord Halifax, thought that he was 'perhaps ultra respectful of public opinion' (Lash, 1977, p. 302), though Roosevelt probably used it as a smokescreen to hide his determination to move at his own pace. He had no wish to shed blood for the sake of it, and moved only as far as the current strategic situation appeared to require. Thus, to Churchill's barely concealed exasperation, he delayed authorizing US Navy escorts for Atlantic convoys until he had absolutely no alternative. His actions suggest, however, that he was determined to get American supplies to Britain, even at the cost of American belligerency. The deteriorating position in the Atlantic therefore pushed him into ever greater intervention, bringing with it inevitable clashes with German U-boats. The Navy steadily widened its Atlantic patrol, the Army occupied Iceland and Greenland to relieve British forces and to deny Germany bases from which to threaten America. By the spring, FDR was confessing, 'I am waiting to be pushed into' a conflict with the U-boats (Burns, 1971, pp. 91–2). In May, he declared a state of unlimited national emergency, warning that 'the war ... is coming very close to home' and that Hitler aimed at world domination (Roosevelt Papers, 1941, p. 185), but still shied away from convoy. Churchill reported from the Newfoundland summit that the President had promised 'everything was to be done to force an incident' in the Atlantic, yet FDR continued to stop short of convoy (Lash, 1977, p. 415). However, in September the USS *Greer*, shadowing a U-boat, provoked a torpedo attack, to which she replied with depth charges. Roosevelt claimed that the 'German submarine fired first upon this American destroyer without warning.' Describing 'these Nazi submarines' as 'the rattlesnakes of the Atlantic', he warned Germany that they risked being sunk on sight in three-quarters of the ocean, concluding prophetically, 'I have no illusions about the gravity of this step' (Roosevelt Papers, 1941, pp. 384, 385, 390, 392). Most significantly, patrol now became convoy; this was undeclared war. An attack on the destroyer *Kearny* (October) brought forth a tone of 'unrelieved belligerency' (Divine, 1969, p. 46) and moral satisfaction: 'the shooting has started. And history has recorded who fired the first shot. America has been attacked' (Roosevelt Papers, 1941, p. 438). However, a substantial element in Congress remained unconvinced by his claims, and it was not until November that he was able to secure the virtual nullification of the neutrality laws by arming merchantmen and sailing them to Britain. Hitler bristled but could go no farther while the Russian campaign continued, and ordered no further provocation of the Americans. By then, however, incidents were impossible to avoid, and Roosevelt's belligerent upholding of American rights ultimately left the decision for war in Hitler's hands. Though FDR hoped to remain at peace, he undoubtedly courted war, and though he carried the nation with him, he was disingenuous. Dallek (1979, p. 289) maintains that, given the country's reluctance to confront Hitlerism squarely, 'it is difficult to fault Roosevelt for building a consensus by devious means.'

Hitler's attack on Russia (June 1941) presented Roosevelt with several problems but also with some opportunities. He had no illusions about Russia's venality and had condemned Stalin's policies in 1939–40. The American people had a rooted aversion to communism and would not be easily persuaded that it was in their interests to aid Russia. Moreover, the German blitzkrieg left Russian survival in doubt. Even if Russia fought on and aid was sanctioned, what remained once other urgent demands were met? Roosevelt's immediate response, though more liberal than Churchill's, was 'sympathetic, expedient and cautious' (Burns, 1971, p. 103). Though some aid was extended almost at once, it was only after Russia had survived the summer that she came under the Lend-Lease umbrella (October 1941). Roosevelt hesitated to exact concessions from Stalin, however, lest he made peace with Hitler; aid, quickened by FDR's personal directive, therefore went to Russia without strings. The Soviet entry into the war was nevertheless not without its advantages. Roosevelt decided that, if the Red Army could engage the bulk of German forces, an American army in Europe might be unnecessary, and in time Russia might help to curb Japanese aggression. As for America's own army, the Selective Service Act, due to expire in October 1941, was renewed only by a one-vote margin in the House, 'a demonstration of how divided and resistant Congress and country remained about entering the war' (Burns, 1971, pp. 277–8).

Meanwhile, America slid into war, equally inexorably, in the Pacific. W. L. Neumann (in Kimball, 1973, p. 73) claimed that it was 'a tragedy of errors', an avoidable conflict brought about by US failure to comprehend the Japanese mind and needs. Reynolds (1981, p. 59) argues that 'The United States had no vital interests in the Far East, and such interests as she did have dictated a conciliatory policy towards Tokyo ... much of America's concern for East Asia sprang from a confused moralizing rather than a hard-headed assessment of US interests.' Roosevelt certainly shared the long-standing American sentimental attachment to China and treated her as a 'ward of court' en route to democracy. Nevertheless, sentiment masked a balanced assessment of American interests. A strong democratic China would inspire Asian colonies demanding independence (a desire fanned by FDR on moral grounds) and check Japanese expansion, while an independent Asia would offer incalculable markets. Chiang's regime still seemed capable of democratization. American support for China, though limited, contrasted with the shameful Anglo-French desertion of Czechoslovakia. Moreover, until the autumn of 1941, Roosevelt's aid to China was restrained enough to permit negotiations with Japan for a Pacific settlement.

After Hitler's 1940 blitzkrieg, however, Japan badgered the defenceless European empires for concessions and, though Roosevelt refused to defend them, he could scarcely avoid an implicit guardianship. It was not in America's interests that Japan should dominate half of the world's people and resources. Thus after Japan moved into French Indo-China, forced Britain to close the Burma Road to China, and harassed the Dutch in the East Indies (summer 1940), Roosevelt abrogated the 1911 American–Japanese commercial treaty. 'The abrogation of the treaty achieved everything the administration could have wished. It encouraged London to be firmer with Tokyo, raised Chinese morale, and received widespread approval in the United States. More importantly, it created anxiety among some Japanese about pushing the United States too hard' (Dallek, 1979, p. 195). Though negotiations continued, Roosevelt's hopes for a settlement were dwindling fast. By July 1941, 'the basic reason the United States was negotiating with Japan was its unreadiness for war'; moreover, 'since Roosevelt expected at any moment to be involved in a shooting war in the Atlantic, his chief concern in the Pacific was to buy time without appearing to back down' (Lash, 1977, pp. 337, 381). Roosevelt still contemplated a meeting with Japan's last civilian premier, though agreement was unlikely and, after a military takeover in October, impossible. By November, American codebreakers knew Japanese forces were poised to move southward. Roosevelt warned Tokyo it might mean war but counselled, 'Let us do nothing to precipitate a crisis'

(Dallek, 1979, p. 305). Talks finally collapsed late in November, with America now resolved to defend Allied colonies and insisting on Japan's withdrawal to the 1931 borders. The Japanese could not lose face, and decided on a desperate gamble to swallow up the South Pacific and South-East Asia, thus presenting America with a fait accompli reversible only at prohibitive cost. Furthermore, by a non-aggression pact signed in Moscow in April 1941, the Japanese had freed themselves of immediate fears of Russian hostility and were thus able to strike southwards. Roosevelt's progressively harder line left him boxed in, as in the Atlantic, though he preferred to say that he had manoeuvred Hitler and Tojo into firing the first shots. War on both fronts was probably unavoidable; America was too powerful and involved to stay out indefinitely. Roosevelt did so as long as he could, but the alternative was a western hemisphere held hostage by the aggressors.

Roosevelt himself offered the best justification for his resistance to Japan: 'We could have compromised with Japan, and bargained for a place in a Japanese-dominated Asia, by selling out the heart's blood of the Chinese people. And we rejected that!' (Roosevelt Papers, 1944, p. 349). Rejection brought a Japanese attack on British, Dutch and American possessions throughout the Pacific, most memorably a brilliant carrier air strike against the American fleet at Pearl Harbor (7 December 1941). The codebreakers knew broadly of Japan's impending moves but not of the air attack on Pearl Harbor; local forces were alerted only against sabotage. Roosevelt and the high command in Washington stand indicted for slack communications and imprecise orders, but it is absolutely untrue that Roosevelt had prior knowledge of the attack. In similar circumstances a British Prime Minister would probably have lost office; Roosevelt relieved the local commanders and otherwise gained the support of a nation at last united, seeking vengeance for a bold but dastardly attack. Defeat for the nation became, ironically, a victory for the President – and for Winston Churchill.

World War II, 1941–1945

Roosevelt referred to 7 December 1941 as 'a date which will live in infamy' (Roosevelt Papers, 1941, p. 514). The next day, requesting a declaration of war against Japan, he remained so unsure of public reaction that he did not include Germany and Italy. Momentarily, his 'Europe First' strategy was in danger, for naturally many now demanded 'Asia First'. However, Hitler and Mussolini, although not formally required to do so by their treaties with Japan, and assuming that the United States would not fight seriously in the Atlantic (Kimball, 1984, I, p. 283), unaccountably declared war on the United States on 11 December, thus freeing Roosevelt from an embarrassing position. Determined on the destruction of the evil empires, he affirmed that 'the United States can accept no result save victory, final and complete' (Roosevelt Papers, 1941, p. 530).

Given Roosevelt's frequent excoriations of the inhuman behaviour of the Axis powers, it is ironic that one of his first wartime acts was to sanction the arbitrary removal of thousands of Japanese-Americans from the Pacific Coast to bleak internment camps in the interior. He bowed to panicky and racist West Coast agitation without giving the matter much thought; he was 'not a strong civil libertarian' (Burns, 1971, p. 216). Though the Japanese were gradually released in 1944, much suffering was caused to innocent people. There are not many stains on the Roosevelt escutcheon; this seems the worst. Nor was Roosevelt's record on European Jews any better than that of other world leaders. Some refugees were accepted from 1938, but it was not a central concern, and the State Department was at best indifferent. Not until it was too late to save many from Hitler's 'final solution' was a more liberal policy adopted (the War Refugee Board, January 1944). Roosevelt saw little hope of rescue and put his faith in a speedy victory in Europe. Dallek's conclusion (1979, p. 168) is just: 'It is difficult to escape the feeling that a sustained call by FDR for allowing Nazi victims to come to the United States in greater numbers might have mobilized the country's more humane instincts ... the Jewish dilemma did not command a very high priority in his mind.' Roosevelt also played down racial tensions within America, refusing effective support for equal opportunities for blacks. Black servicemen continued to suffer the same extensive discrimination, gratuitous violence, and complete segregation within the forces which had persisted since the Civil War; though some token desegregation took place from 1944, not until a decade after a war against racism were the services fully desegregated.

Roosevelt's principal wartime role, by circumstances and choice, was as Commander in Chief. He became 'a real and not merely a nominal Commander in Chief ... few Presidents have shared Mr. Roosevelt's readiness to exercise it in fact and in detail with such determination' (M. Watson, in Lash, 1977, p. 397). His long-standing interest in strategy, his World War I experience, his 'Roosevel-tian' activism and his frustrated military ambition contributed to his enthusiasm for the role; as Burns comments, he 'lived it' (1971, p. 491). FDR began to organize and personally control America's defences from the summer of 1939. However, when war broke out, one British general commented that 'the whole organisation belongs to the days of George Washington' (Larrabee, 1987, p. 17). Early in 1942, Roosevelt streamlined the high command, eliminating duplication, integrating bureaux and replacing commanders. Admiral Leahy, a former Chief of Naval Operations and ex-ambassador to Vichy France, became Chief of Staff to the Commander in Chief and effectively chairman of the newly created Joint Chiefs of Staff. Roosevelt also copied Churchill's 'Map Room', a graphic war information centre.

The President faced a situation no less disastrous than that of 1933. 'The whole South Pacific defense was in disarray,' notes Burns (1971, p. 209), war production lagged, the army was still incapable of major overseas operations, many of the latest aircraft were going to the Allies and the navy was shaken by Pearl Harbor. Roosevelt rallied and roused the nation. The daring if militarily meaningless bombing raid on Tokyo (April 1942), an example of 'Roosevelt's instinct for audacity' (Larrabee, 1987, p. 365) was one result. The tough, capable Admiral Ernest J. King (he was said to shave with a blowlamp) became Chief of Naval Operations. Appointing Admiral Nimitz to the Pacific command, Roosevelt ordered: 'Tell Nimitz to get the hell out to Pearl and stay there til the war is won' (Larrabee, 1987, p. 354). Shrewd and aggressive, he was, like almost all of FDR's appointments, an excellent choice. Roosevelt's knack of finding outstanding commanders was exemplified by his selection of General George C. Marshall as Army Chief of Staff in 1939, 'one of the finest and most consequential choices of his presidency' (Larrabee, 1987, p. 96). Universally acknowledged as a man of transcendent strategic and organizational ability, rugged integrity and evident authority, Marshall was never an intimate of FDR (he objected to the President referring to the Navy as 'us' and the Army as 'them'). Nevertheless, he earned both Roosevelt's and Churchill's deep respect; it is debatable whether there was a greater man in uniform on the Allied side.

Roosevelt's chief strategic concern was 'to defeat the Axis through the maximum possible use of American industrial power, but with the minimum possible expenditure of American lives' (Gaddis, 1972, p. 65). He purposely concentrated on the quickest, most direct route to victory, eschewing details about the postwar settlement until victory had been achieved. Roosevelt, wrote Welles, had 'a grasp of the principles of geopolitics' which was 'almost instinctive' (Dallek, 1979, p. 321) and was confident of his ability to judge priorities. After Pearl Harbor, however, Churchill, fearful that Roosevelt might be stampeded into a 'Pacific First' strategy, hurried to Washington. He need not have worried. Roosevelt took the opportunity to insist upon the Anglo-American Combined Chiefs of Staff being headquartered in Washington, and also pressed for a decisive invasion of Europe in 1942. Churchill blanched at the thought of a green Allied army, inadequately supported, assaulting Fortress Europa. Even if the invaders were not repelled on the beaches, a Great War-style trench warfare might ensue; no British cabinet could survive the onset of another war of attrition. Churchill countered with proposals for the strategic bombing of Germany, a tighter blockade and peripheral operations in the Mediterranean. Roosevelt was prepared to concede that the Western allies might not be able to invade France in 1942. He was insistent, however, that an American army should engage the Germans somewhere in that year, and despite the opposition of his military advisers, who objected to the diversion of forces from the build-up for the Normandy landings, he suggested what became the 'Torch' operation which liberated North Africa in the winter of 1942–3. It was a well justified decision. The Americans gained valuable experience in a theatre where mistakes would not be catastrophic. Furthermore, a workable Anglo-American military command was evolved. It is but a slight exaggeration to say that D-Day was won in the battles in North Africa.

FDR had swung away from an exclusively maritime strategy towards one favouring air power in 1937. His 10,000-plane programme rose to 50,000 in 1942 and 125,000 in 1943. A great day-bomber force in Britain co-operated with the RAF's night bombers, and when the B-29, a true strategic bomber (Larrabee, 1987), was projected, Roosevelt quickly saw its potential for destroying Japan from Pacific island bases, and put his authority behind it. In October 1939 he had been told about the possibility of an atomic bomb; fearing the Germans might get it first and grasping its awesome potential, he authorized Anglo-American co-operation on what became known as the Manhattan Project, and ordered unlimited resources for it. The atomic understanding with Britain was confirmed by the Hyde Park Agreement of 1943.

In early 1942 the urgent need was to stem the Japanese advance, which was halted by the great American victory in the carrier battle of Midway (June 1942). The Americans thereafter assumed the offensive, invading Guadalcanal; when commanders debated withdrawal, Roosevelt insisted that they hang on. Devoting up to a third of their forces to the Pacific, the Americans pursued an astonishingly successful 'whipsaw' strategy (Larrabee, 1987), with Nimitz chasing the Japanese homeward on a northerly course and General Douglas MacArthur directing a more southerly drive, culminating in the reconquest of the Philippines (1944). MacArthur, 'an essentially thespian general' (Larrabee, 1987, p. 350), was a 'political' appointee in that, according to Larrabee, he was the darling of conservatives and isolationists; loosing him on the Japanese enabled FDR to satisfy these would-be critics and keep a potential troublemaker well away from home. Roosevelt thus 'saw to it that MacArthur's ego was gratified' (Larrabee, 1987, p. 351).

Following the North African triumph, Roosevelt and Churchill met at Casablanca (January 1943), having failed to persuade Stalin to leave Russia. Intent on keeping their forces active and on relieving the Russians (facing three-quarters of Germany's army), they agreed to invade Sicily in the spring and looked forward to a second front in 1944 (a delay which disgusted Stalin). Most importantly, Roosevelt announced a policy of 'unconditional surrender'. He desired to avoid an armistice like that of 1918, as a result of which Hitler had claimed that Germany had not been defeated. He has been criticized for inciting the German people to fight to the bitter end, but it is unlikely that the policy had a significant effect. It certainly expressed widespread Allied opinion. At Quebec in September 1943, FDR and Churchill agreed on an American Supreme Commander for the proposed cross-Channel invasion, and on a supporting landing in southern France, and organized a South East Asia Command. However, the British still hesitated to invade France, opposed the diversion of troops from Italy and advocated a Balkan offensive. Fundamental and unresolved Anglo-American disagreements were not uncommon, despite the genuinely friendly relationship FDR enjoyed with Churchill. The Americans pressed for the dismantling of Empire Preference, sought to prevent Britain rebuilding her gold and dollar reserves, opposed the revival of her export trade during the war and spoke of cutting back Lend-Lease after D-Day (June 1944), while particularly fierce rows broke out over world air routes and Britain's home food production and imports. America ultimately grudgingly agreed to continue Lend-Lease until the end of the war, but a two-year postwar loan came with stiff terms (Dobson, 1986). As Dobson observes (p. 185), 'The riddle that the British Government had to solve was how to get America's help without incurring dollar liabilities and becoming more vulnerable to political and economic pressure from her.' It is only fair to say that FDR was considerably more generous than some of his grasping subordinates, but he endorsed the general policy of undermining Britain's world trading position.

Roosevelt's most serious clash with Churchill came over the future of colonialism. He had launched the Philippines on the path to independence in 1934 and advocated worldwide decolonization. He hoped to prevent the French re-occupation of Indo-China and he favoured the return of Hong Kong to China. His principal target for freedom, however, was India. Roosevelt jousted intermittently against Churchill's 'profound and reactionary imperialism' (Thorne, 1978, p. 669) and pressed the Prime Minister to assure India of postwar independence in return for a secure base against Japan. American special missions aroused false hopes in the Indians and, to put it mildly, exasperated the British. Roosevelt's whole approach to this complex problem was extremely simplistic, but he continued to press Churchill on the matter, though without success.

Roosevelt also suspected that the British wished to dominate Western Europe. There was, says Thorne (1978, p. 109), an 'underlying American belief that Britain was inclined to play the international game according to a different, dangerous and corrupt set of rules from those observed by a disinterested and enlightened United States'. In particular, America distrusted traditional European 'balance of power' and 'spheres of influence' politics. 'American foreign policy from Wilson to Roosevelt,' notes Kimball (1984, p. 14), 'had constituted a radical critique of international relations as conducted by the European powers.' Thus when Churchill sought to prevent Communist domination in Italy and Greece (and to establish British influence), Roosevelt, with some justice, doubted his motives and gave only grudging and tardy support. 'The Anglo-American relationship was ... remarkably close and yet particularly strained,' writes Thorne (1978, p. 150). However, 'A key aspect of the Churchill–Roosevelt relationship was the candid, friendly, informal atmosphere that both men worked to create and preserve' (Kimball, 1984, p. 3). Their relationship reached its peak at the Quebec conference of 1943. Thereafter, America's might overshadowed Britain's contribution, and FDR now expected Churchill to follow his lead. Moreover, with Italy defeated, the Japanese irretrievably on the run and the Russians driving irresistibly to the heart of Europe, Churchill, Roosevelt and Stalin met together (for the first time) at Tehran (November 1943) to discuss the coming peace. Roosevelt's Lend-Lease Administrator, Leo Crowley, observed that 'The Roosevelt–Stalin axis is gaining strength and the Roosevelt–Churchill axis is losing strength in about equal ratio' (Thorne, 1978, p. 276). The era of the superpowers had begun.

The omens for a fruitful Roosevelt–Stalin relationship were poor. Anglo-American supplies to Russia were subject to stoppages and shortages, and Roosevelt had rashly promised an invasion of Europe in 1942. Anglo-American anxiety to relieve Russia was genuine but Stalin could be forgiven for suspecting that the West wanted the Nazis and the Communists to destroy each other. 'The second front delay far more than any other factor aroused Soviet anger and cynicism' (Burns, 1971, p. 374). Nevertheless, at Tehran Roosevelt set out to charm Stalin, in his own mind successfully: 'I "got along fine" with Marshal Stalin ... I believe that we are going to get along very well with him' (Roosevelt Papers, 1943, p. 558). It is doubtful whether Stalin was charmed, but it suited him to co-operate, confirming Russian participation against Japan after Hitler's defeat, abolishing the Comintern, renouncing world revolution and promising to launch an offensive to coincide with the invasion of France (then scheduled for May 1944). Tehran seemed a fitting climax to a year of Allied victories and improved relations (Smith, 1965).

Cold War shadows were nevertheless present. The Russians, from the darkest days of the German invasion, had consistently looked ahead to a victorious peace, demanding Western recognition for the re-absorption of the Baltic republics and of Finnish territory, and for a western border at the expense of Poland, and friendly neighbouring governments. Roosevelt was in a dilemma; the American people supported democracy and self-determination in central Europe, yet FDR knew that the Russian steamroller would roll inexorably over the area. He hid this fact from his people and cultivated a trusting relationship with Stalin, suggesting a postwar Grand Alliance and a United Nations, delaying settlements until victory was achieved. Roosevelt consistently overestimated his success at unfreezing Stalin. The Russian leader's resentment at Anglo-American prevarication, suspicion of their aims, and his own determination to control central Europe, remained. He displayed little interest in a United Nations and a postwar Grand Alliance, and rejected Roosevelt's proposal for plebiscites in the Baltic republics. He demanded harsh terms and a comprehensive occupation for Germany, but was happy to leave the details to the foreign ministers. The real sticking point, however, was Poland, which Stalin wanted under his thumb. Roosevelt secured a delay on Poland until after the 1944 Presidential election, telling Stalin that he dared not face millions of Polish-American voters with an unfavourable agreement (thus implying that a favourable one was unlikely). Indeed, he had accepted a Churchill–Stalin agreement of October 1944 to divide the Balkans into British and Soviet spheres of influence and 'had cautiously indicated to the Russians that they could count on a free hand in Eastern Europe' (Gaddis, 1972, p. 134). Furthermore, he proposed to withdraw American forces from Europe within two years of victory.

For the time being, however, Roosevelt could ignore these distasteful realities and savour the American triumphs of 1944. The American economy, less than fully stretched, churned out almost half of the world's armaments, and though government administration of the war effort was somewhat haphazard, FDR played a vital role as 'a creative and energizing agent' (Perkins, 1947, p. 308). The White House now sheltered a powerful, pervasive and permanent bureaucracy; the 'imperial presidency' was emerging. Effective presidential control of the outsize 'palace guard' became impossible, and FDR himself concentrated on the direction of military operations. The problems inherent in the growth of executive power were then insignificant, however, compared with a string of sunlit victories in both Pacific and European theatres. Among these, the successful invasion of Western Europe stands paramount. Roosevelt had selected General Dwight D. Eisenhower to weld together the multinational combined operation, which took place on D-Day (6 June 1944) because 'he was the best politician among the military men' (Larrabee, 1987, p. 438). The President was mightily relieved when the landings succeeded.

Major issues of war and peace nevertheless remained to be resolved, and in August 1944 Roosevelt and Churchill met again at

Quebec. Churchill once again pressed for a Balkan offensive to forestall a Russian seizure of the northern shores of the Mediterranean; Roosevelt, though never totally rejecting the idea, agreed only to step up the Italian campaign. He also stalled on Churchill's request that he should recognize de Gaulle as France's leader and grant France occupation zones in Austria and Germany. As for Germany itself, both men supported the drastic Morgenthau plan to deindustrialize Germany, but American opinion was outraged and Roosevelt executed a nimble retreat. American policy on Germany remained in hopeless confusion – tough and lenient schemes were under simultaneous discussion, Roosevelt characteristically postponing a decision until forced to make one. Churchill did score one success at Quebec. He was anxious that after Hitler's defeat British forces should liberate their Asian empire themselves and play a significant part in the Pacific war. FDR overcame his staff's objections and welcomed a substantial British contribution to the final campaigns against Japan.

Until Britain and Russia could shift their main forces from Europe, the principal American ally in the Far East was China. Roosevelt and a sceptical Churchill had met Chiang Kai-shek at Cairo in November 1943, en route to Tehran. America's 'favourite ally' (Dallek, 1979, p. 329) remained an enigma throughout the war. China tied down considerable Japanese forces, offered bases for air and amphibious attacks on Japan and might fill the Far Eastern power vacuum after Japan's defeat. In his meetings with Chiang, Roosevelt therefore flattered the Generalissimo, renounced American extra-territorial rights, re-opened Chinese immigration, promised the return of all territories seized by Japan since 1894, and dangled the possibilities of the return of Hong Kong and Stalin's recognition of the Nationalist regime. Nevertheless, he deftly sidestepped Chiang's demands for more American supplies; China still came bottom of the list. In fact, Roosevelt alternately encouraged and chided Chiang, attempting to extract military action in return for more aid. Chiang, unresponsive but grasping, was content to let the Americans win the war for him while he built up his forces for the impending struggle with Mao's Communists. However, 'No amount of evidence concerning Chiang's maladministration, the disunity of the country, the strength of the opposition, or the inefficiency of the Kuomintang's armies appeared capable of shaking Roosevelt's illusions, at least until the closing months of the war' (Smith, in Kimball, 1973, p. 179). By 1944, Chiang was politically and militarily bankrupt, and the successful Pacific strategy rendered China largely irrelevant to the defeat of Japan; Roosevelt rapidly lost faith in his protégé. 'Of all the allies of the United States China excited the highest hopes and ultimately proved the most crushing disappointment' (Smith, 1965, p. 6). Roosevelt's obsession with China as a great power did little damage during the war but contributed greatly to America's traumatic shock when China repudiated her guidance in favour of communism in 1949 – ironically the event which in due course brought China true great power status.

The progress of Allied arms elsewhere in the world in 1944–5 forced Roosevelt to make decisions about postwar policies which he had hitherto avoided. Following the Italian surrender in September 1943, he adopted a pragmatic stance. 'I don't care with whom we deal in Italy,' he declared, 'so long as it is not a definite member of the Fascist Government... The first thing is to avoid anarchy... You can't get self-determination in the first week that they lay down their arms. In other words, common sense' (Roosevelt Papers, 1943, pp. 344–5). The substantial Italian-American vote made lenient treatment sound politics. A similar pragmatism ultimately prevailed in his policy towards France. Though FDR despised France's pre-war policy, desired the dismemberment of her empire and doubted that she could regain great power status, the liberation of Paris (August 1944) placed de Gaulle so firmly in control of France that Roosevelt was at last compelled to recognize him. Nevertheless, he still hoped to ease the French (and the British) out of their positions in the Middle East, and believed that if he could remove the European powers, he could mediate between the region's Muslims, Christians and Jews (Smith, 1965). Having come to appreciate the complexity of the Middle Eastern situation, he avoided pledging support for the Zionist cause, despite his awareness of the substantial Jewish vote at home.

Roosevelt hoped that the world's postwar problems could be solved by a blend of great power co-operation and a new world organization. He had clung privately to his League convictions, yet he was no simple Wilsonian, combining Wilson's idealism with TR's *realpolitik*. His United Nations was to be dominated by 'Four Policemen' – the United States, Britain, Russia and China. Each would assure the peace on its own 'beat' – America's was the Western Hemisphere – and there would be 'police stations' manned by the forces of a 'Policeman' at strategic points such as

Gibraltar, Dakar and Okinawa. This Grand Alliance in peacetime mode would dominate the United Nations Security Council by virtue of permanent seats. 'Little countries would be required to keep quiet and take orders' (Smith, in Kimball, 1973, p. 180). The UN's Charter was essentially the Atlantic Charter, signed by over twenty nations early in 1942, pledging widespread freedom, self-determination and collective security. Churchill, though alarmed at the implications for the empire, had little choice but to go along with Roosevelt. Stalin, an unenthusiastic recruit, demanded a UN vote for each of the sixteen Soviet republics. FDR kept this quiet and beat Stalin down to three. Stalin also demanded Big Four unanimity on the Security Council, but settled for a veto.

Stalin was easier to persuade than the US Senate, the Republicans and the isolationists (Gaddis, 1972). FDR worked skilfully and assiduously to prepare his people for their new role. In 1942, he had warned them, 'We shall have to take the responsibility for world collaboration, or we shall have to bear the responsibility for another world conflict' – a direct echo of Wilson (Roosevelt Papers, 1942, p. 585). In 1944, he announced, 'The power which this nation has attained ... has brought us the responsibility, and with it the opportunity, for leadership in the community of Nations.' He dared to declare, 'The Council of the United Nations must have power to act quickly and decisively to keep the peace by force, if necessary' and (even bolder) 'if the world organization is to have any reality at all, our American representative must be endowed in advance ... with the authority to act.' This was the crucial point on which Wilson's League fell before the Senate in 1919–20. Roosevelt was confident the UN would not do so, for 'the American people had become ... a seasoned and mature people' (Roosevelt Papers, 1944, pp. 349, 350, 354). Indeed, each step to assuring American membership in and leadership of the United Nations consciously avoided Wilson's false footsteps. Roosevelt courted the Republicans, placing their former isolationist spokesman, Senator Vandenberg, on the American delegation to the UN's inaugural meeting at San Francisco (April 1945). 'This strategy of bipartisanship paid off handsomely when the UN Charter came before the Senate on July 28, 1945 – it passed by a vote of 89–2' (Gaddis, 1972, p. 30). No one knew how precisely the reality would accord with the ideal, but Roosevelt's hopes were fervent and undimmed. 'The tragedy of war,' wrote Sherwood (1948, p. 225), 'was always somewhere within the rim of his consciousness.'

The climactic meeting with Stalin and Churchill came at Yalta (February 1945). Much remained to be settled: Russian intervention against Japan; Poland's government and boundaries; and the occupation of Germany. American service chiefs still insisted on the necessity for Soviet participation against Japan. In return, Stalin exacted railway and port concessions in China, and claimed the return of Russian territory lost to Japan in 1905. These demands breached the Open Door and Chinese territorial integrity and sovereignty yet again, though Stalin did deign to recognize the Nationalist government. It was a bad deal for both China and America (made worse by being negotiated by Roosevelt on the absent Chiang's behalf), yet given the current military appreciation and Russia's ability to flow into the space vacated by Japan, Roosevelt had little choice but to agree to it.

The powers agreed that Nazism must be extirpated from Germany, drew up occupation zones, and divided Berlin between them (granting France shares). Reparations, boundaries and war criminals were left to the foreign ministers. More importantly, Western access to Berlin, deep in the Soviet zone, was not laid down in unequivocal terms, an ambiguity which contributed to the crisis of 1948–9, when the Russians closed the land routes. Ultimately, 'efforts to work out tripartite policies for Germany ... failed largely because of conflict and confusion within the United States Government' (Gaddis, 1972, p. 96). Roosevelt's sometimes muddled approach to hard problems and his aversion to detail served the West ill in this case. FDR did secure a sonorous 'Declaration on Liberated Europe', involving 'interim governments broadly representative of all democratic elements in the population ... (followed by) free elections'. Spheres of influence were declared to be 'incompatible with the basic principles of international collaboration' (Roosevelt Papers, 1945, pp. 534, 579). This clashed with the Churchill–Stalin division of influence in the Balkans (to which Roosevelt had agreed with misgivings).

Roosevelt's ideals were tested most sharply over Poland, in which all three powers had strong interests. Britain had ostensibly gone to war for Polish independence in 1939 and now harboured an exile government. Roosevelt, committed to the principle of self-determination, courted his Polish voters. The Russians, however, held the most vital stake. A long-standing enmity marked Russian–Polish relations, and Russia had suffered three invasions via Poland. Stalin was determined to regain his Nazi–Soviet Pact share of pre-war

Poland and to install a Communist-dominated government in Warsaw, based principally on the exile cabinet he had sponsored in Lublin. The London and Lublin 'governments' would hardly speak to each other, and the London Poles haughtily rejected Anglo-American advice to accept Russia's boundary claim; they were not mollified by the offer of compensation in the west at Germany's expense. In 1943, Polish accusations of a Russian massacre of Poles in Katyn Forest prompted Stalin to break off relations with the London group. In the summer of 1944, despite Anglo-American entreaties, he refused to help the Warsaw rising against the Germans or to co-operate with Western air supply efforts. After the rising's collapse, the Red Army swarmed across Poland; Stalin was in possession of the field.

At Yalta, the Allies agreed that 'the provisional government which is now functioning in Poland should therefore be reorganised on a broader democratic basis with the inclusion of democratic leaders from Poland itself and from Poles abroad.' They were 'pledged to the holding of free and unfettered elections as soon as possible'. It represented 'the most hopeful agreement possible for a free, independent and prosperous Polish state' (Roosevelt Papers, 1945, pp. 535, 583). Stalin 'did not desire Poland to be an appendage of' Russia and hoped the two nations would be 'good neighbors' (Roosevelt Papers, 1944, p. 160). Roosevelt had apparently secured his demands but recognized that realization depended upon Stalin's goodwill. Shortly after Yalta, however, Stalin's Lublin puppets ignored the pledge of free elections and imposed a Communist government. Could Roosevelt have done more to save Poland? He might have exploited Stalin's desperate need for assistance in 1941, but few Westerners then saw Russia as the future threat, and he feared that strong demands would force Stalin into a quick peace with Hitler (Welles, in Kimball, 1973). He should certainly have prepared the American people for the possible destruction of their hopes instead of selling them an unattainable dream. The bickering London Poles, who refused 'to do the practical thing' (Roosevelt Papers, 1944, p. 160) and accept the proposed borders and a marriage with Lublin, did not help themselves. However, it is difficult to see what could have prevented Russia from filling the vacuum left by Germany in Eastern Europe. 'The fate of Poland,' writes Smith (1965, p. 137), 'symbolised the collapse of the dream of Allied unity and the beginning of ... open and ominous conflict between Russia and the West.'

Smith attributes Roosevelt's failure at Yalta to physical and mental deterioration. 'President Roosevelt was a dying man at Yalta ... The power of the President's mind had also declined in the months since Tehran ... He seemed eager to patch together quick agreements' (1965, p. 131). Roosevelt was tired, less attentive, at times seemingly vacant and less resilient. Nevertheless, he seems to have been in normal form at Yalta (Burns, 1971; Dallek, 1979) and he knew that the West lacked the power to secure a better result. Increasingly alarmed from the summer of 1944 about Russian intentions, he listened more to hardliners, and he and Churchill had agreed in 1943 not to furnish Russia with atomic secrets until her co-operation in Europe was guaranteed (Smith, 1965). Developing a policy of 'accommodation with firmness' after Yalta (Dallek, 1979, p. 527), Roosevelt excluded Russia from Anglo-American negotiations to secure a German surrender in Italy, riding Stalin's wrath but counselling that the incident should be forgotten in the interests of postwar amity. Roosevelt's chief objectives throughout the war were to keep Russia fighting, to avoid premature postwar settlements, and to rely on the United Nations to assuage Russian security fears and determine the postwar world scene. As Burns observes (1971, p. 546), 'he found the right formula for getting the most militarily from the Russians without letting them ... occupy the whole continent' – though there is little indication that Stalin wanted any more than he obtained. Diane Clemens (in Kimball, 1973, p. 195) states that 'considering the favorable military position of the Soviet Union ... [it] showed a cooperative and conciliatory stance' and that it was the West which reneged on Yalta. Western and Eastern definitions of freedom, friendliness, elections and self-determination differed sharply; each side could accuse the other of repudiating the agreements. Stalin seems to have granted the West a face-saving accord at Yalta and was then surprised that the Americans took it seriously and accused him of bad faith. Burns's verdict is the fairest: 'He [Roosevelt] had reached the limit of his bargaining power at Yalta. His position resulted not from naïveté, ignorance, illness, or perfidy, but from his acceptance of the facts' (1971, p. 572).

A further sign that the Grand Alliance was coming apart was Stalin's rejection of an American postwar loan, preferring a bootstraps recovery to humiliating conditions. (American economic might fell harshly on Britain, however, in the stringent terms of the loan negotiated by Keynes in 1946.) Roosevelt had identified economic nationalism as a prime cause of the Great Depression, and sought the universal adoption of the Open Door principle, confident of America's ability to profit from it the most. In July 1944, the Roosevelt administration sponsored the International Monetary Fund and the World Bank to ensure a sound recovery and expansion. 'In effect,' concludes Gardner, it 'offered the world a modernized international gold standard complete with a replacement for the old international banking system' and represented 'a New Deal in international economics' (1964, pp. 284–5).

It is arguable whether the United States ended the war with 'less national security than in 1941' (Smith, 1965, p. 173), but there was little Roosevelt could have done to prevent America's postwar insecurity. The Americans were certainly insensitive to Soviet needs, but Stalin's paranoia ultimately contributed greatly to the breakdown of the Grand Alliance, and Hitler's defeat sealed its fate, for a common antipathy to Nazism remained its only bond. The end of the war brought centre against periphery in a classic strategic confrontation, later given greater acuteness by the development of mutual nuclear mass-destruction capability.

As a warlord, Roosevelt had the priceless quality of being 'calm and composed' and 'buoyant'; he 'can sleep anywhere', wrote his secretary Bill Hassett (Burns, 1971, pp. 298–9). He also had the capacity to keep to 'the larger objectives and not get bogged down in argument over methods and details' (Burns, 1971, p. 358). Churchill regarded him as 'the most skilful strategist of them all' (Larrabee, 1987, p. 644) because of his great synoptic and intuitive grasp of the war. He had a happy knack of selecting and then inspiring outstanding commanders, fitting the man to the task with exactitude. 'His conduct as Commander in Chief,' concludes Larrabee, 'bears the mark of greatness' (1987, p. 644). Victory came in 1945 much as he willed it – complete, cheaply for the Americans, and with his people at last willing to play their true role in world affairs. For Franklin Roosevelt, however, peace came too late. On 12 April 1945, three months into his fourth term, just past his sixty-third birthday, two weeks before the United Nations' inaugural meeting, three weeks before Germany surrendered, and with the atomic bomb poised, on Roosevelt's own decisive order, over Japan, the President died at his retreat in Warm Springs, Georgia, of a massive brain haemorrhage. After the shock, the world stood back to assess the achievement of one of history's most successful and powerful figures.

Conclusion

Franklin D. Roosevelt, by general consent, stands next to Lincoln in the presidential pantheon, but wherein lies his greatness?

As President, FDR displayed characteristics instilled in his Hyde Park childhood and youth. That tranquil, detached, quaint rural background endowed him with a remarkable capacity for relaxation and a self-assurance lightly worn. His essentially self-contained childhood and family circumstances developed in him an eagerness to please, a persistence shading into stubbornness, a well honed deviousness and a determination to play his cards so close to his chest as to make him the despair of generations of politicians (and biographers). 'I could never really understand what was going on in there,' remarked Sherwood (1948, p. 10). To these hereditary and environmental legacies, Roosevelt added in the 1920s, following his polio attack, a physical and moral courage revealed dramatically in his calm demeanour in the wake of the Miami assassination attempt when he was President-elect. The same fortitude characterized his leadership in the dark days of 1933 and 1941, and communicated itself to the nation.

Debate continues as to how deliberate was his entry into politics, but once in the field, he proved a quick learner, rapidly developing a vigorous campaigning style and consciously cultivating a distinctive identity while capitalizing astutely on the name and fame of Theodore Roosevelt. Both Roosevelts were hyperactive, always in search of the limelight, incapable of inaction in the face of challenge. FDR consciously prepared himself to succeed TR as the clan chieftain, and 'the White House was for him almost a family seat' (Neustadt, 1964, pp. 154–5). Though FDR was for much of his time completely informal, he could assume a dignity as regal as it was natural. As TR's self-annointed heir, FDR identified himself with the great presidential traditions. He adopted, with the innocence born of spiritual kinship, the lineage of Washington, Jefferson, Jackson, Lincoln, cousin Theodore and his own chief, Woodrow Wilson. These men made, remade or expanded the Presidency, and were therefore innovators, as was FDR; but their innovation was consciously within strict parameters, an enhancement rather than a repudiation of the essentially conservative American political tradition. FDR was no exception; the transformation of government and foreign policy during his reign notwithstanding, he adhered to Macaulay's dictum: 'Reform if you would preserve.' 'You have made yourself,' wrote Keynes, 'the trustee for those in every country who seek to mend the evils of our condition by reasoned experiment within the framework of the existing social system' (in Schlesinger, 1960, p. 656). Franklin Roosevelt was the exemplar of the middle way as much from conviction as from political calculation. His guide was intuition rather than reason, yet his political philosophy is identifiable, for he alluded to it on numerous occasions. In affirming constantly that he sought the greatest happiness of the greatest number and that he believed in the freedom of the individual up to the point at which it might harm the community, he demonstrated his allegiance to John Stuart Mill's refined Utilitarianism. The ascription would have caused him to wrinkle his nose, raise his eyebrows and smile a wry but incurious smile.

Roosevelt had an intuitive grasp of the pluralist nature of American politics and was a natural harmonizer and coalition builder. He cultivated a constant dialogue with the people; his finger was rarely far from the nation's pulse. To his almost supernal political intuition was allied an acute sense of timing equally transcendent. Burns has aptly described him as both a lion and a fox, alternately displaying courage and cunning. Lover of power though he was, nevertheless he was no mere opportunist. Power in his hands was meant to serve noble purposes. At home, his central aim was to ensure to all Americans the security, happiness and fulfilment he had experienced. Abroad, his vision was of one world, enjoying peace, prosperity and the blessings of liberty which he had championed so vigorously at home during the New Deal. His ambitions for America and the world were only partially fulfilled, as much because of his own shortcomings as of circumstances beyond his control. Political calculation handicapped a resolute drive to banish depression and distribute equitably the fruits of an economy of abundance. Overconfidence in the applicability of domestic

References

Adams, D.K. 1982: Paper given at Roosevelt Centenary Conference, Keele University.

Army and Navy Journal, 22 May 1915.

Badger, A.J. 1982: Paper given at Roosevelt Centenary Conference, Keele University.

Baskerville, S.W. and Willett, R. (eds) 1986: *Nothing Else to Fear: New Perspectives on America in the Thirties*. Manchester: Manchester University Press.

Bernstein, B.J. (ed.) 1970: *Towards a New Past: Dissenting Essays in American History*. London: Chatto and Windus.

Braeman, J., Bremner, R. and Walters, E. (eds) 1964: *Continuity and Change in the Twentieth Century*. Columbus: Ohio State University Press.

Braeman, J., Bremner, R. and Walters, E. (eds) 1975: *The New Deal*: vol. 1, *The National Level*; vol. 2, *The State and Local Levels*. Columbus: Ohio State University Press.

Burns, J.M. 1956: *Roosevelt: The Lion and the Fox, 1882–1940*. New York: Harcourt Brace.

Burns, J.M. 1971: *Roosevelt: The Soldier of Freedom, 1940–1945*. London: Weidenfeld and Nicolson.

Cole, W.S. 1983: *Roosevelt and the Isolationists, 1932–1945*. Lincoln: University of Nebraska Press.

Conkin, P.K. 1967: *FDR and the Origins of the Welfare State*. New York: Crowell.

Dallek, R. 1979: *Franklin D. Roosevelt and American Foreign Policy, 1932–1945*. New York: Oxford University Press.

Daniels, J. (ed. Cronon, E.D.) 1963: *The Cabinet Diaries of Josephus Daniels*. Lincoln: University of Nebraska Press.

Davis, K.S. 1972–86: *FDR*, 3 vols, to 1937. New York: Random House.

Divine, R.A. 1962: *The Illusion of Neutrality*. Chicago: University of Chicago Press.

Divine, R.A. 1969: *Roosevelt and World War II*. Baltimore: Johns Hopkins University Press.

Dobson, A.P. 1986: *U.S. Wartime Aid to Britain, 1940–1946*. London: Croom-Helm.

Farley, J. A. 1948: *Jim Farley's Story*. New York: Whittlesey House.

Freidel, F. B. 1952–73: *Franklin D. Roosevelt*, 4 vols. Boston: Little, Brown.

Freidel, F. B. (ed.) 1964: *The New Deal and the American People*. Englewood Cliffs: Prentice-Hall.

Gaddis, J. L. 1972: *The United States and the Origins of the Cold War, 1941–1947*. New York: Columbia University Press.

Gardner, L. C. 1964: *Economic Aspects of New Deal Diplomacy*. Madison: University of Wisconsin Press.

Gardner, L. C. 1970: *Architects of Illusion: Men and Ideas in American Foreign Policy, 1941–1949*. Chicago: Quadrangle Books.

Garraty, J. A. (ed.) 1970: *Interpreting American History*, vol. 2. London: Collier-Macmillan.

Garraty, J. A. 1986: *The Great Depression*. New York: Harcourt Brace.

Hareven, T. K. 1968: *Eleanor Roosevelt: An American Conscience*. Chicago: Quadrangle Books.

Hofstadter, R. 1955: *The Age of Reform*. New York: Vintage.

Hofstadter, R. 1967: *The American Political Tradition*. London: Cape.

Ickes, H. L. 1953–4: *The Secret Diary of Harold L. Ickes*, 3 vols. New York: Simon and Schuster.

Kimball, W. F. 1969: *'The Most Unsordid Act': Lend-Lease, 1939–1941*. Baltimore: Johns Hopkins University Press.

Kimball, W. F. (ed.) 1973: *Franklin D. Roosevelt and the World Crisis, 1937–1945*. Lexington, Mass.: Heath.

Kimball, W. F. (ed.) 1984: *Churchill and Roosevelt: the Complete Correspondence*, 3 vols. Princeton: Princeton University Press.

Larrabee, E. J. 1987: *Commander in Chief*. London: Deutsch.

Lash, J. P. 1977: *Roosevelt and Churchill, 1939–1941: The Partnership that Saved the West*. London: Deutsch.

Leopold, R. W. 1962: *The Growth of American Foreign Policy*. New York: Knopf.

Leuchtenburg, W. E. 1963: *Franklin D. Roosevelt and the New Deal, 1932–1940*. New York: Harper.

Leuchtenburg, W. E. 1964: 'The New Deal and the Analogue of War'. In Braeman et al. 1964: *Continuity and Change in the Twentieth Century*. Columbus: Ohio State University Press.

McElvaine, R. S. 1983: *Down and Out in the Great Depression: Letters from the Forgotten Man*. Chapel Hill: University of North Carolina Press.

McElvaine, R. S. 1984: *The Great Depression*. New York: Times Books.

Moley, R. 1939: *After Seven Years*. New York: Harper.

Morgan, T. 1985: *FDR: A Biography*. New York: Simon and Schuster.

Neustadt, R. 1964: *Presidential Power*. New York: Mentor.

Patterson, J. T. 1967: *Congressional Conservatism and the New Deal*. Lexington, Kentucky: University of Kentucky Press.

Pells, R. 1973: *Radical Visions and American Dreams: Cultural and Social Thought in the Depression Years*. New York: Harper.

Perkins, F. 1947: *The Roosevelt I Knew*. London: Hamish Hamilton.

Reynolds, D. 1981: *The Creation of the Anglo-American Alliance, 1937–1941: A Study in Competitive Cooperation*. London: Europa.

Rollins, A. B., Jr. 1962: *Roosevelt and Howe*. New York: Knopf.

Romasco, A. U. 1983: *The Politics of Recovery: Roosevelt's New Deal*. New York: Oxford University Press.

Roosevelt, Eleanor 1949: *This I Remember*. New York: Harper.

Roosevelt, Elliott (ed.) 1948: *FDR: His Personal Letters*, 3 vols. New York: Duell, Sloan and Pierce.

Rosen, E. A. 1977: *Hoover, Roosevelt and the Brains Trust*. New York: Columbia University Press.

Rosenman, S. I. (ed.) 1937– : *The Public Papers and Addresses of Franklin D. Roosevelt, 1928–1945*, 14 vols. Various US publishers.

Rosenman, S. I. 1952: *Working with Roosevelt*. London: Hart-Davis.

Schlesinger, A. M., Jr. 1956–60: *The Age of Roosevelt*, 3 vols. Boston: Houghton Mifflin.

Sherwood, R. E. 1948: *The White House Papers of Harry L. Hopkins*. London: Eyre and Spottiswoode.

Sitkoff, H. 1978: *A New Deal for Blacks: The Emergence of Civil Rights as a National Issue: The Depression Decade*. New York: Oxford University Press.

Smith, G. 1965: *American Diplomacy during the Second World War*. New York: Wiley.

Thorne, C. 1978: *Allies of a Kind: The United States, Britain and the War Against Japan, 1941–1945*. Oxford: Oxford University Press.

Trout, C. H. 1977: *Boston, the Great Depression and the New Deal*. New York: Oxford University Press.

Tugwell, R. G. 1968: *The Brains Trust*. New York: Viking.

Tugwell, R. G. 1969 (originally published 1957): *The Democratic Roosevelt*. Baltimore, Penguin.

Ward, G. C. 1985: *Before the Trumpet: Young FDR, 1882–1905*. New York: Harper.

Ware, S. 1981: *Beyond Suffrage: Women in the New Deal*. Cambridge, Mass.: Harvard University Press.

Ware, S. 1982: *Holding Their Own: American Women in the 1930's*. Boston: Twayne.

Notes on Further Reading

Most of the books listed are American publications but those in print are obtainable in Britain and all titles should be available in good academic libraries. Where British publishers are listed, it usually means that the British edition is a year later than the American edition. Several books have gone through second editions or reprints; the details given are for the editions used in this study.

Contemporary Works

The principal source is S. I. Rosenman (ed.), *The Public Papers and Addresses of Franklin D. Roosevelt, 1928–1945*, 14 vols (various US publishers from 1937). Rosenman has also left a modest but vivid memoir, *Working With Roosevelt* (London: Hart-Davis, 1952). Elliott Roosevelt (ed.), *FDR: His Personal Letters*, 3 vols (New York: Duell, Sloan and Pierce, 1948) is especially useful for 1913–28, and a mature perspective on the immature FDR is Josephus Daniels in E. D. Cronon (ed.), *The Cabinet Diaries of Josephus Daniels* (Lincoln: University of Nebraska Press, 1963). The best documentary collection on the New Deal is W. E. Leuchtenburg (ed.), *The New Deal: A Documentary History* (New York: Harper, 1968), and another quite comprehensive selection is F. B. Freidel (ed.), *The New Deal and the American People* (Englewood Cliffs: Prentice Hall, 1964). A vivid perspective on those who suffered most is given in R. S. McElvaine, *Down and Out in the Great Depression: Letters from the Forgotten Man* (Chapel Hill: University of North Carolina Press, 1983). FDR's unusually articulate associates have left many memoirs, among which are: J. A. Farley, *Jim Farley's Story* (New York: Whittlesey House, 1948), by FDR's political manager; Raymond Moley, *After Seven Years* (New York: Harper, 1939), by his chief Brains Truster, later an acute if slightly jaundiced critic; Frances Perkins, *The Roosevelt I Knew* (London: Hamish Hamilton, 1947), an intensely human portrait and excellent on social issues. Harold L. Ickes, *The Secret Diary of Harold L. Ickes, 1933–1941*, 3 vols (New York: Simon and Schuster, 1953–4) can be waspish but has the virtues of freshness and, from 1936, an insider's view. R. E. Sherwood, *The White House Papers of*

Harry L. Hopkins, 1939–1946, 2 vols (London: Eyre and Spottiswoode, 1948) is especially valuable for the wartime years, when Hopkins was FDR's most trusted lieutenant. A. B. Rollins, Jr., *Roosevelt and Howe* (New York: Knopf, 1962) is a biographical study crucial to understanding the 1912–33 era. Eleanor Roosevelt, *This I Remember* (New York: Harper, 1949) is very much a 'family' memoir but with a number of valuable political points.

Biographies

The best life is by J. M. Burns, *Roosevelt: The Lion and the Fox, 1882–1940* (New York: Harcourt Brace, 1956) and *Roosevelt: The Soldier of Freedom, 1940–1945* (London: Weidenfeld and Nicolson, 1971) elegantly written and a particularly incisive analysis of the problems of leadership in a democracy. The most exhaustive and lucid treatment, down to the end of 1933, is F. B. Freidel, *Franklin D. Roosevelt*, 4 vols (Boston: Little, Brown, 1952–73). R. G. Tugwell, *The Democratic Roosevelt* (Baltimore: Penguin, 1969; originally published 1957) by a Brains Truster, is a deeply reflective study. Gracefully written and more penetrative than any other is G. C. Ward, *Before the Trumpet: Young FDR, 1882–1905* (New York: Harper, 1985); he is now at work on a volume going down to 1928. Other recent studies are Ted Morgan, *FDR: A Biography* (New York: Simon and Schuster, 1985), rather more 'our hero with feet of clay' than most; and K. S. Davis, *FDR*, 3 vols, to 1937 (New York: Random House, 1972–86), detailed but highly readable. T. K. Hareven, *Eleanor Roosevelt: An American Conscience* (Chicago: Quadrangle Books, 1968) is the best biography of the First Lady.

The New Deal

The outstanding history is W. E. Leuchtenburg, *Franklin D. Roosevelt and the New Deal, 1932–1940* (New York: Harper, 1963), erudite, comprehensive, succinct and compulsive reading. A. J. Badger is completing a new study (London: Macmillian). D. K. Adams, *Franklin D. Roosevelt and the New Deal* (London: Historical Association, 1979) is an excellent synthesis, particularly good on the philosophy of the New Deal. A. U. Romasco, *The Politics of Recovery: Roosevelt's New Deal* (New York: Oxford University Press, 1983) is a penetrating discourse on the political economy of the New Deal. R. Pells, *Radical Visions and American Dreams: Cultural and Social Thought in the Depression Years* (New York: Harper, 1973) is perceptive on the interaction of politics and culture. A. M. Schlesinger, Jr., *The Age of Roosevelt*, 3 vols (Boston: Houghton Mifflin, 1956–60) is brilliantly written, rather inclined to compartmentalize but with excellent vignettes. W. E. Leuchtenburg answers major questions about the New Deal in J. A. Garraty, *Interpreting American History*, vol. 2 (London: Collier-Macmillan,

1970). Garraty has placed the New Deal in international perspective in *The Great Depression* (New York: Harcourt Brace, 1986). Leuchtenburg has an important essay, 'The New Deal and the Analogue of War' in J. Braeman et al., *Continuity and Change in the Twentieth Century* (Columbus: Ohio State University Press, 1964). J. Braeman et al., *The New Deal*, vol. 1, *The National Level*, and vol. 2, *The State and Local Levels* (Columbus: Ohio State University Press, 1975) has many fine essays, notably on blacks, business, agriculture and labour. On the Brains Trust, R. G. Tugwell, *The Brains Trust* (New York: Viking, 1968) is by a former member, while Raymond Moley, assisted by E. A. Rosen, *The First New Deal* (New York: Harcourt Brace, 1966) is good on the First Hundred Days. Rosen, *Hoover, Roosevelt and the Brains Trust* (New York: Columbia University Press, 1977) is particularly acute and valuable on the election and interregnum of 1932–3. B. J. Bernstein, 'The New Deal: the Conservative Achievements of Liberal Reform' in Bernstein (ed.), *Towards a New Past: Dissenting Essays in American History* (London: Chatto and Windus, 1970) is one of the few radical critiques. R. S. McElvaine, *The Great Depression* (New York: Times Books, 1984) is a very comprehensive treatment of the whole decade. S. W. Baskerville and R. Willett have edited a very strong collection of British essays, *Nothing Else to Fear: New Perspectives on America in the Thirties* (Manchester: Manchester University Press, 1986). P. K. Conkin, *FDR and the Origins of the Welfare State* (New York: Crowell, 1967) is marvellously compressed, scintillating and incisive. R. Hofstadter, *The Age of Reform* (New York: Vintage, 1955) is equally stimulating, relating the New Deal to Populism and Progressivism; his essay on FDR in *The American Political Tradition* (London: Cape, 1967) is pithy and profound. C. H. Trout, *Boston, the Great Depression and the New Deal* (New York: Oxford University Press, 1977) is an excellent study of the difficulties the New Deal encountered at local level. R. Neustadt, *Presidential Power* (New York: Mentor, 1964) is a classic dissection. On blacks, see particularly H. Sitkoff, *A New Deal for Blacks: The Emergence of Civil Rights as a National Issue: The Depression Decade* (New York: Oxford University Press, 1978); and on women, S. Ware, *Beyond Suffrage: Women in the New Deal* (Cambridge, Mass.: Harvard University Press, 1981) and *Holding Their Own: American Women in the 1930's* (Boston: Twayne, 1982). J. D. Lees, *The President and the Supreme Court: New Deal to Watergate* and J. T. Patterson, *The Welfare State in America* (both British Association for American Studies pamphlets, 1980 and 1981 respectively) are excellent brief syntheses. I have benefited greatly from the papers given at the Roosevelt Centenary Conference at Keele University (1982), especially those by D. K. Adams and A. J. Badger. J. T. Patterson, *Congressional Conservatism and the New Deal* (Lexington, Kentucky: University of Kentucky Press, 1967) is a carefully crafted analysis. H. Ickstadt, R. Kroes and B. Lee (eds), *The Thirties: Politics and Culture in a Time of Broken Dreams* (Amsterdam: Free University Press, 1987) is an extremely useful volume of essays by Dutch, West German, American and British scholars.

The best general survey of American foreign policy is R. W. Leopold, *The Growth of American Foreign Policy* (New York: Knopf, 1962), well organized, thoughtful and balanced. The standard work on FDR is R. Dallek, *Franklin D. Roosevelt and American Foreign Policy, 1932–1945* (New York: Oxford University Press, 1979), exhaustive and judicious. Equally thorough is W. S. Cole, *Roosevelt and the Isolationists, 1932–1945* (Lincoln: University of Nebraska Press, 1983). R. A. Divine, stimulating if controversial, has four books on FDR: *The Illusion of Neutrality* (Chicago: University of Chicago Press, 1962); *The Reluctant Belligerent: American Entry into World War II, 1939–1941* (New York: Wiley, 1965); *Roosevelt and World War II* (Baltimore: Johns Hopkins University Press, 1969), the most contentious book; and *Second Chance: The Triumph of Internationalism in America during World War II* (New York: Atheneum, 1971). The *Roosevelt Papers* and the biographies are immensely useful, too. On Anglo-American relations, D. Reynolds, *The Creation of the Anglo-American Alliance, 1937–1941: A Study in Competitive Cooperation* (London: Europa, 1981) is outstanding, dispelling cosy myths of unrelieved harmony, as does A. P. Dobson, *U.S. Wartime Aid to Britain, 1940–1946* (London: Croom Helm, 1986) a lucid, comprehensive yet compact dissection. J. P. Lash, *Roosevelt and Churchill, 1939–1941: The Partnership that Saved the West* (London: Deutsch, 1977) romanticizes slightly but is generally trenchant and always well written. W. F. Kimball, *Churchill and Roosevelt: the Complete Correspondence*, 3 vols (Princeton: Princeton University Press, 1984), is a major contribution to scholarship and has a particularly perspicacious introduction. He has edited a very broad selection of views on FDR's later policy, *Franklin D. Roosevelt and the World Crisis, 1937–1945* (Lexington, Mass.: Heath, 1973). America's role in World War II is well surveyed by A. R. Buchanan, *The United States and World War II*, 2 vols (New York: Harper, 1964). E. J. Larrabee, *Commander in Chief* (London: Deutsch, 1987) has searching essays on FDR and his senior commanders. G. Smith, *American Diplomacy during the Second World War* (New York: Wiley, 1965) is a clear, brief treatment. On the origins of the Cold War, see particularly J. L. Gaddis, *The United States and the Origins of the Cold War, 1941–1947* (New York: Columbia University Press, 1972), a well balanced assessment, and L. C. Gardner, *Architects of Illusion: Men and Ideas in American Foreign Policy, 1941–1949* (Chicago: Quadrangle Books, 1970), a 'New Left' critique. Gardner has also written a fine study of Open Door economic policy, *Economic Aspects of New Deal Diplomacy* (Madison: University of Wisconsin Press, 1964). C. Thorne, *Allies of a Kind: The United States, Britain and the War Against Japan, 1941–1945* (Oxford: Oxford University Press, 1978) is a challenging and penetrating analysis, broader than the title suggests. W. F. Kimball, *'The Most Unsordid Act': Lend-Lease, 1939–1941* (Baltimore: Johns Hopkins University Press, 1969) is a precise and succinct analysis.

GI Bill of Rights, 46
Glass-Steagall Banking Act, 26
gold standard, 31–2
Good Neighbor policy, 50, 51, 53
Grand Alliance, 70, 73, 76, 77
Great Depression, 17, 18, 20, 22, 23, 28, 32, 47, 49, 51, 77
greenbelt cities, 36

Halifax, Lord, 60
Hitler, Adolf, 46, 54, 56, 57, 60, 61, 62, 63, 64, 67, 69, 71, 75, 77
Home Owners' Loan Corporation, 26, 31
Hong Kong, 68, 71
Hoover, Herbert C., 15, 19–20, 21, 22, 24, 32, 50
'Hoovervilles', 21, 22
Hopkins, Harry L., 18, 26, 35, 36, 44, 45–6, 58
House of Representatives, 19, 39, 45, 55, 61
Housing Act (1937), 43
Howe, Louis McHenry, 5, 6, 8, 11, 13, 40, 44
Hughes, Chief Justice Charles Evans, 41–3
Hyde Park Agreement, 67

Ickes, Harold L., 22, 30, 40
India, 68
Indo-China, 62, 68
industry, 20, 25, 29–30, 41
inflation, 10, 11, 24, 32, 33, 34
International Monetary Fund, 77
internationalism, 10–12, 31, 50, 58, 61, 63, 70–7, 80
interregnum (1932–3), 21–2
investment, 26, 31, 33, 44, 48
isolationism, 11, 12, 50, 51, 52, 53, 54, 55, 56, 58, 67, 73
Italy, 9, 52–3, 56, 57, 63, 67, 68, 69, 71, 72, 76

Japan, 7, 50, 52, 53, 54, 55, 59, 61–4, 66, 67, 68, 69, 71, 72, 74, 77
Jews, 12, 39, 64, 72
Johnson, Hugh S., 20–1, 29, 30

Keynes, John Maynard, 43, 44, 76, 79
King, Admiral Ernest J., 65

labour: conditions, 4, 16, 20, 22, 29, 30, 35, 40, 43; unions, 1, 5, 8, 11, 27, 29, 30, 32, 33, 37, 38, 39, 41, 43, 48
Landon, Alfred M., 39
Latin America, 7, 50, 51, 53
League of Nations, 10–12, 50, 51, 52, 72, 73
Leahy, Admiral William D., 65
Lend-Lease, 58–9, 61, 68, 69
Liberty League, 33
Lindbergh, Charles, 58
London Economic Conference, 32
London Naval Conference (1935), 53
Long, Huey P., 34–5, 39
Ludlow Amendment, 55

MacArthur, General Douglas, 34, 67
Manchuria, 50
Manhattan Project, 66–7
Mao Tse-tung, 71

Marshall, General George C., 65
Mediterranean, 66, 67, 71
'merchants of death', 52, 53
Middle East, 72
Moley, Raymond, 17, 19, 21, 22
Monroe Doctrine, 7, 50
Morgenthau, Henry, Jr., 17, 44, 71
Mussolini, Benito, 56, 57, 64

National Industrial Recovery Act, 27, 33. 41
National Labor Relations Act, 37, 42
National Recovery Administration, 27, 29, 38, 40, 43
National Resources Committee, 36
National Union for Social Justice, 34–5
National Youth Administration, 36, 40
Navy, US, 2, 6–11, 12, 13, 51, 53, 54, 55, 57, 60, 65
Nazi–Soviet Pact, 56, 74
Nazism, 54, 64, 69, 74, 77
neutrality, US: 1914–17, 7, 52; 1935–41, 52, 53, 55, 56, 57, 60–1
New Deal, 1, 20, 23–49, 51, 77, 79, 80
Newfoundland conference, 59, 60
New York: city, 1, 2–3, 9, 18; Governorship, 10, 12, 14, 15–18, 46; state, 3–6, 8, 10, 12, 14, 15–18, 26, 37, 46; State Senate, 3–6
Nimitz, Admiral Chester W., 65, 67
non-recognition doctrine, 50, 51, 54

O'Connor, Basil (Doc), 19
Old Age Revolving Pensions, 35
Open Door policy, 50, 74, 77

peace movement, 7, 50, 52, 53, 54, 55, 57–8
Pearl Harbor, 50, 63, 65, 66
pensions, 16, 17, 35, 36, 38, 47
Perkins, Frances, 5, 15, 16, 17, 22, 26, 36, 40
Philippines, 67, 68
Pittman, Key, 56
planning, 25, 29, 31, 35, 36
Poland, 56, 69, 70, 74–5
Preparedness campaign, 6–7
Presidency, 5, 11, 14, 15, 16, 17, 18, 20, 27, 28, 43, 45, 48, 70, 78, 79, 80
progressivism, 4, 5, 11, 12, 15, 16, 22, 26, 35, 38, 39, 40, 41, 42, 44–5, 51, 53, 79–80
Prohibition, 12, 15, 20, 24
public works, 17, 20, 26, 27, 29, 30, 44
Public Works Administration, 26, 27, 29, 30
Public Utilities Holding Companies Act, 37, 38
Pure Food and Drug Act, 43
Purge of Democratic Party, 44–5

'quarantine' speech, 54–5
Quebec conferences: 1943, 67, 69; 1944, 70–1

radicalism, 22, 24, 34–5, 38, 39
Reciprocal Trade Agreements Act, 31
Reconstruction Finance Corporation, 26–7, 31
Reorganization Bill, 43
Republican Party, 3, 4, 5, 7, 11, 12, 14, 15, 16, 17, 18, 20, 22, 25, 31, 32, 39, 42, 43, 44, 45, 46, 50, 58, 73

89

Resettlement Administration, 36, 43
Roosevelt, Eleanor, 3, 13, 17, 40–1
Roosevelt, Franklin Delano: assassination
    attempt, 22, 78; beginning in politics, 3;
    childhood, 1–2; Commander in Chief, 64–
    5, 70, 77; conclusions about, 78–80; death
    of, 77; economic policies, 19, 20, 22, 29–
    30, 31–2, 43–4, 47, 48, 67, 76, 79, 80;
    education, 2, 13, 19; as election
    campaigner, 3–6, 8, 12, 15–16, 18–21,
    38–41, 46, 58, 70, 78; family background,
    1–3; and farming, 1, 4, 5, 16, 20, 25–6, 29,
    31, 39; financial views, 3, 17–18, 24, 25,
    32, 43–4; and foreign policy, 7, 9, 11–12,
    45, 46, 50–77, 79–80; in interregnum
    (1932–3), 21–2; first inauguration, 23; and
    First World War, 6–10; marriage, 3, 13,
    17, 40–1; personality, 2, 3, 5–6, 12, 13, 19,
    28, 78; philosophy, 1, 3, 4, 6, 12, 28, 30,
    35, 38, 47, 48, 49, 78–80; physical decline,
    76; polio, 13–14, 15–16, 78; presidential
    campaigns: 1932, 18–21; 1936, 38–41;
    1940, 46, 58; 1944, 46, 70; and the press,
    5, 6, 10, 11, 12, 23; and radio, 16, 19–20,
    24; and rearmament, 6–7, 26, 45, 51, 53,
    55, 57, 59, 65; relationship with public, 21,
    23–4, 32, 39, 46, 49, 54, 58, 60, 78, 79;
    religion, 2; Roosevelt coalition, 28, 39, 46,
    48, 79; Roosevelt recession, 43–4, 48; and
    Second World War, 30, 32, 56–77, 80; as
    State Senator, 3–6; and strategy, 7–8, 19,
    51, 55, 56, 59, 60, 64, 65–6, 67, 77, 80;
    Vice-Presidential campaign, 11–12; war
    aims, 59, 65–6, 67–8, 71, 72–7, 80
Roosevelt, James, 1, 2
Roosevelt, Sara Delano, 1, 2, 3
Roosevelt, Theodore, 3, 4, 6, 7, 38, 51, 72,
    78, 79
Rosenman, Samuel I., 15, 19
Rumsey, Mary Harriman, 40
Rural Electrification Administration, 31

Securities and Exchange Commission, 31, 38
Selective Service Act, 61
Senate: New York State, 3–6; US, 4, 8, 10,
    11, 12, 34, 37, 39, 45, 52, 56, 58, 73
'Share Our Wealth', 34
sharecroppers, 34, 38, 47
Schecter case, 41, 42
Sinclair, Upton, 33
Smith, Alfred E., 14, 15–16, 20, 33
social security, 20, 35, 36, 38, 40, 42, 44
Social Security Act, 36, 38, 40, 42
Socialist Party, US, 22
Southern Tenant Farmers' Union, 34
Soviet Union, 52, 56, 61, 63, 67, 69, 70, 71,
    72, 74, 75, 76, 77

Spanish Civil War, 53
Stalin, Joseph, 56, 61, 67, 69, 70, 71, 73, 74,
    75, 76, 77
subsistence homesteads programme, 36
Summers, Hatton, 42
Supreme Court, 41–3

Tammany Hall, 4, 5, 8
tariff, 13, 20, 31
taxation, 17, 25, 29, 32, 33, 35, 36–7, 38,
    41
Tehran conference, 69, 71, 76
Temporary Emergency Relief Administration,
    17–18
Temporary National Economic Committee,
    43
Tennessee Valley Authority, 25, 28, 31, 40,
    41
Townsend, Dr Francis, 34–5, 39
Truman, Harry S., 46
Truth-in-Securities Act, 20, 26, 31
Tugwell, Rexford G., 19, 36

unconditional surrender, 64, 67
unemployment: figures, 17, 21, 23, 26, 29, 43,
    47; compensation, 17, 36; relief, 17, 20, 21,
    22, 24, 25, 26, 28, 30–1, 32, 35, 38, 39, 40,
    44, 47, 48
Union Party, 39
United Nations, 70, 72–3, 76, 77

Wagner, Robert F., 37
Wall Street, 2, 17, 31, 37
Wallace, Henry A., 22, 46
War Industries Board, 27
War Refugee Board, 64
wars: Spanish-American, 7; First World War,
    6–10, 28, 29, 52, 65, 66; Second World
    War, 30, 32, 56–77, 80
welfare state, 26, 36, 38, 40, 46, 48, 49,
    80
Welles, Sumner, 56, 66
Western Hemisphere, 6, 50, 51, 53, 57, 63,
    72
Willkie, Wendell L., 46, 58
Wilson, Woodrow, 4, 5, 6, 7, 9, 10, 11, 38, 50,
    51, 52, 55, 68, 72, 73, 79
women, 4, 22, 31, 38, 40–1
Works Progress Administration, 35, 38
World Bank, 77
World Court, 51, 52
World Disarmament Conference, 50

Vandenberg, Arthur H., 73

Yalta conference, 74–6

Zionism, 72